EX LIBRIS

A SUSSEX GUIDE

SUSSEX
WRITERS
& ARTISTS

EDWARD LUCIE-SMITH

Illustrated by
IVAN HISSEY

SNAKE RIVER PRESS

SNAKE RIVER PRESS

Book No 2
Books about Sussex for the enthusiast

Published in 2007 by
SNAKE RIVER PRESS
South Downs Way, Alfriston, Sussex BN26 5XW
www.snakeriverpress.co.uk

ISBN 978-1-906022-01-3

This book was conceived, designed and produced by
SNAKE RIVER PRESS

ART DIRECTOR & PUBLISHER *Peter Bridgewater*
EDITORIAL DIRECTOR *Viv Croot*
EDITOR *Robert Yarham*
PAGE MAKEUP *Richard Constable & Chris Morris*
ILLUSTRATOR *Ivan Hissey*
CONSULTANT *Lorraine Harrison*

This book is typeset in Perpetua & Gill Sans,
two fonts designed by Eric Gill

Printed and bound in China

———

CONTENTS

INTRODUCTION

'And there shall the Sussex songs be sung
And the story of Sussex told'.
HILAIRE BELLOC, *THE SOUTH COUNTRY*

The 41 brief biographies printed here offer a picture of a very special part of England, one which has long been celebrated for its physical beauty. They also have something to tell us about the way English society has changed and developed. Until quite recently, Sussex, which we now think of as being easily accessible, was quite remote. Any ambitious creative person, intent on making his or her mark in the world, needed to get away, and go to London. This was the case with the Elizabethan and Jacobean statesman, Thomas Sackville, part author of *Gorboduc*, the earliest blank verse play in English, and a prototype for Shakespeare's King Lear. It was also the case with the 17th-century dramatist Thomas Otway, born near Chichester, whose *Venice Preserv'd* is the only Restoration-period tragedy – as opposed to Restoration comedy – that is still occasionally revived.

Things only started to change in the early 19th century, when Brighton attracted the attention of the Prince Regent and started to be developed as a seaside-resort. From the very beginning, however, this development was seen as a corrupting influence, as can be seen from John Constable's remarks on the subject, quoted in this book. Yet it is doubtful that Constable would have cared to go there if Brighton had not become famous, not only because of the Regent's presence, but because of the new fashion for sea-bathing, which had supposedly curative powers. Constable's much-loved wife Maria was suffering from consumption, and the couple went to Brighton hoping for a cure.

Brighton built up a reputation not only as a place of amusement, but as a town whose sleaziness and squalor could on occasion match that of London. One can see this reflected in two forceful novels – Graham Greene's *Brighton Rock*, which was made into a memorable film, and Patrick Hamilton's sinister *The West Pier*. There are also glimpses, and more than glimpses, of squalid urban life in Robert Tressell's *The Ragged Trousered Philanthropists*, which is set in Hastings.

The Sussex countryside became a refuge for writers and artists, but particularly for writers, in the early years of the 20th century. Among the well-known writers who settled there, or had weekend homes there, were Henry James, Kipling, Conan Doyle, Hilaire Belloc and Virginia Woolf. All of these had already established their literary reputations before they found homes in Sussex. Some did not write about Sussex at all – James is an example – some, on the other hand, were keen to celebrate it as a part of 'Old England', a kind of rural paradise. There was, however, something intrinsically artificial about this celebration – this is really the point of Stella Gibbons's *Cold Comfort Farm*, which is one of the funniest books ever written, a satire on every rural cliché ever committed to paper. Gibbons was aware that the relationship between the apparently remote and tranquil Sussex countryside and the bustling, competitive world of literary London was symbiotic. Novels and poems about rural Sussex were essentially addressed to an urban audience.

One way of trying to solve this problem was to write about Sussex for children, which was the choice made by A.A. Milne in his books about Winnie the Pooh and in his poems about his son Christopher Robin. Yet there is something ambiguous about these texts. They offer adults a nostalgic vision of what childhood is like without, I think entering into the world of childhood with complete conviction. It is not surprising, that Milne's son grew to hate his father's work, and to wish that Milne had refrained from using his real name.

There is, of course, an important difference between what writers want from the countryside and what artists want. Writers want tranquility, freedom from interruption and freedom from urban noise and bustle. Painters want something they can paint – and when they have exhausted a particular range of subject-matter, they move on. This was the case with nearly all of the artists discussed here, that is, if they painted specifically 'Sussex' subjects, such as landscapes. Quite a few of them didn't. William Blake, Edward Burne-Jones and Eric Gill all lived and worked in Sussex for substantial periods, but there is little or no immediately recognizable trace of Sussex in what they produced. The only painter who celebrated Sussex throughout the larger part of his career – and he is, it must be said, an attractive artist of only the second rank – was Ivon Hitchens.

In fact, if one wants to see the impact of Sussex on one of the major geniuses of English art – indeed some people would call him the greatest genius of them all – one has to look at the pre-modern epoch, and, specifically, at the paintings and drawings that J.M.W. Turner made at Petworth. And here there is a further paradox: the park at Petworth, which Turner celebrated so lyrically in his paintings, was an artificial creation. It had been reshaped totally between 1751 and 1757 by the great landscape gardener Lancelot 'Capability' Brown – that is to say, 70 years before Turner started work there in 1828.

The park at Petworth is a reminder that Sussex is not simply a work of unaided nature, which human beings, at some particular stage in their existence, are privileged to enjoy. Its appearance and its unique atmosphere are things that have been shaped by the presence of creative people. This is particularly true of the history of the county from the beginning of the 19th century onwards. Improved transportation was one of the things that made the fortune of Brighton as a fashionable seaside resort, and it was improved transportation that made it possible for creative people to consider living in various parts of rural Sussex, either full time or part time. Very few of them had much genuine experience of the English countryside before they got there, and nearly all of those who wrote about Sussex, or depicted its landscape, tended to idealize its qualities as a kind of paradise – a process visible in the writing of Kipling, Belloc and even of A.A. Milne. This is why Stella Gibbons's wonderful satire *Cold Comfort Farm* is such a necessary corrective. Yet few people would think of Gibbons as a 'typically Sussex writer', just as few think of Turner as a 'typically Sussex painter'. In fact, part of the fascination of the biographies that follow is the way in which they demonstrate that Sussex, as a place, is not only very various in itself, but has played host to a wide, and ultimately unclassifiable, variety of creative impulses.

Each biography is accompanied by a short list of recommended books to read or pictures to see. In some cases, these are the only works of the writer or artist in question. We have tried to focus on work that has a Sussex connection, however tenuous, but ultimately the choices are subjective, intended to be an introductory taster for readers who have not come across the writer or artist in question before.

THE
BIOGRAPHIES

DAISY ASHFORD

1881-1972

LEWES

Daisy Ashford, without a doubt now one of the best-known Sussex authors, wrote her celebrated book *The Young Visiters* in 1890, when she was only nine years old and living in Lewes. The manuscript lay in a drawer for nearly 30 years, until it was finally published in 1919, with a preface by J.M. Barrie. Speaking of the photograph of the child-author that accompanied the text, Barrie wrote:

> *This is no portrait of a writer who had to burn the oil at midnight (indeed there is documentary evidence that she was hauled off to bed every evening at six): it has an air of careless power; there is a complacency about it that by the severe might perhaps be called smugness. It needed no effort for that face to knock off a masterpiece.*

In fact the sheer confidence of the narrative – a child's eye view of English upper-class society – and what seemed to be its sharp satirical edge caused many people to believe that the text had been written by James Barrie himself.

Though *The Young Visiters* is not – contrary to report – the only novel or novella that Daisy produced (there was another one called *The Hangman's Daughter*, in addition to a number of short stories). She stopped writing when she was in her teens, though, according to her daughter, she continued to tell entertaining stories – invented lives for people she had observed in a teashop or elsewhere. But when her masterpiece was finally published, she couldn't see what all the fuss was about, or why her book had become an instant classic. Since its publication, it has never been out of print.

Its immediate success was partly due to the cult of childhood that flourished in Britain in the years immediately after World War I, perhaps in reaction to the horrors of the war itself. A.A. Milne's Pooh stories and poems featuring his son Christopher Robin were beneficiaries of the same impulse – a need to try to reclaim a lost innocence. There was also the fact that *The Young Visiters*, with its naïve but telling vision of Victorian high society, recalled something that suddenly seemed incredibly exotic and remote.

One reason for the book's continued popularity, however, is that it is stuffed with quotable quotes. For example, who can forget Daisy's child's-eye vision of royalty? 'Here on a golden chair was seated the prince of Wales in a lovely ermine cloak and a small but costly crown.' And other gems are not difficult to find: 'Bernard always had a few prayers in the hall and some whiskey afterwards as he was rather pious.' Or, 'My own idear [sic] is that these things are as piffle before the wind.'

In her own way, Daisy was a phrase-maker on a par with Oscar Wilde.

Ashford's Top Works
- *The Young Visiters, 1919*
- *Love and Marriage (with Angela Ashford), 1965*
- *The Hangman's Daughter, 1983*

ENID BAGNOLD
1889-1981

ROTTINGDEAN

Enid Bagnold is remembered for two very different literary works – her novel *National Velvet* (*1935*), which was the basis for the successful film of the same name (*1944*), and which kick-started the career of the then very young Elizabeth Taylor; and also for her rather static and literary play *The Chalk Garden* (*1956*), which provided starring roles for two major actresses, dames Edith Evans and Peggy Ashcroft.

Born in Kent in 1889, Bagnold spent part of her childhood in Jamaica, but was educated in England and in Switzerland. She then went to art school in London, and lost her virginity (as she later recorded in a book of memoirs) to the famously predatory writer Frank Harris. The event took place in a traditional setting for such things – a private room at the Café Royal in London.

During World War I Bagnold worked as a nurse, and was dismissed for writing a pamphlet critical of the administration of the hospital where she was employed – the Royal Herbert Hospital in Woolwich, which looked after soldiers who had been wounded in France. Later she served in France, as a driver.

In 1920 she married Sir Roderick Jones, head of the Reuters News Agency, and in 1923 the couple bought North End House in Rottingdean, which had been the home of the painter Sir Edward Burne-Jones (*see p. 30*). Later, they extended their quarters by buying The Elms, a house once occupied by Rudyard Kipling (*see p. 58*), before he moved to Burwash. The Joneses had a family of four children. The children's involvement with and success in local gymkhanas provided the inspiration for *National Velvet*, which is about a 14-year-old girl called Velvet Brown, who wins a piebald horse in a raffle and who, disguised as a boy, triumphs in the Grand National. Many of the characters in the book were closely based on local people.

The setting for *The Chalk Garden* is recognizably the Garden Room at North End House.

Partly because of Sir Roderick Jones's job, but also thanks to her own activity as an author, Bagnold knew a large number of celebrities, about whom she was not always kind. She had a major row with Cecil Beaton, when his set-designs for the New York production of *The Chalk Garden* were not re-used in London, and they did not speak to one another for 20 years thereafter. Kipling, with whom in theory at least she was on friendly terms, Bagnold dismissed as 'a little man whom nobody knew well' and as 'a quite unconscious homosexual'. One reason for her volatile reactions may have been the fact that she became a life-long morphine addict, after a hip-operation.

⌒⌒⌒

Bagnold's Top Works
- ❯ *Serena Blandish, 1924*
- ❯ *National Velvet, 1935*
- ❯ *The Chalk Garden, 1956*

AUBREY BEARDSLEY
1 8 7 2 - 9 8

BRIGHTON

It seems appropriate that Aubrey Beardsley was born in Brighton. The Pavilion, although neglected by Queen Victoria as being too reminiscent of the raffish days of her uncle George IV, still survived in 1872, the year of his birth, and supplied a touch of the exoticism that was to colour all of Beardsley's work.

The Beardsleys were middle-class but poor, as Aubrey's father Vincent had frittered away the family fortune. Both Aubrey and his sister Mabel were regarded as infant prodigies, but there was little money to spend on their upbringing. In addition, Aubrey's health was always precarious. At the age of nine he suffered his first tubercular attack.

Beardsley attended Brighton Grammar School as a boarder, and his first literary and artistic efforts were published in *Past and Present*, the school magazine – first, in 1885, a poem called *The Valiant*, then, in the following year, a series of drawings called *The Jubilee Cricket Analysis*. In 1888 he supplied the drawings for the programme of the school's Christmas play, which was called *The Pay of the Piper*.

None of these efforts caused much of a stir. Beardsley's big break came when he moved to London in 1889, where he worked as an insurance clerk. He and his sister called uninvited at Burne-Jones's London studio. A servant sent them away, but the artist, catching a glimpse of Mabel's red hair, called them back and looked at Beardsley's portfolio, which was full of Burne-Jones-style drawings. Impressed by what he saw, the older artist encouraged Beardsley to take night classes at Westminster Art School.

By 1893 Beardsley was established as an illustrator, first with his drawings for a new edition of Malory's *La Morte d'Arthur*, then, in 1894, with a set of fantastic illustrations for Oscar Wilde's play *Salome*. He briefly became the art editor of *The Yellow Book*, the periodical that epitomized the success of the Decadent Movement in England. Although Oscar Wilde never contributed to *The Yellow Book*, his trial and disgrace tainted Beardsley's reputation. A slightly disreputable publisher called Leonard Smithers created a new magazine for him called *The Savoy*, and gave him classic texts to illustrate, among them Alexander Pope's mock-heroic epic poem, *The Rape of the Lock*.

By this time Beardsley's health was deteriorating fast, and he could not sustain the pace Smithers imposed on him. He moved to the South of France in 1895, and died there in March 1898 at the age of 25, after a death-bed conversion to Catholicism.

Beardsley's Top Works
- *Le Morte d'Arthur, 1893-4*
- *Oscar Wilde's 'Salome', 1894*
- *Aristophanes 'Lysistrata', 1896*

Bell's Top Works (see next page)
- *Virginia Woolf, 1911-12*
- *The Tub, 1917*
- *Interior with Table, 1921*

VANESSA BELL
1879-1961

CHARLESTON

Vanessa Bell was the eldest child of Sir Leslie Stephen, by his second marriage to Julia Duckworth. She studied at the Royal Academy Schools, then at the Slade. After the death of her some-what overwhelming father in 1904, she moved, with her younger sister Virginia (*see p. 89*) and her brothers Thoby and Adrian, to Gordon Square in London. Thoby's friends from Cambridge began to frequent the house and the 'Bloomsbury Group' was formed.

In 1907 Vanessa married the art critic Clive Bell (she had previously refused him twice, but changed her mind after her brother Thoby died suddenly from typhoid fever) and had two sons by him, Julian (*1908-37*), killed when working as an ambulance driver for the Republican side in the Spanish Civil War, and Quentin (*1910-1997*). In 1910 she met the painter and critic Roger Fry, when he came to speak at the 'Friday Club', a regular gathering she had founded to bring progressive artists and writers together.

In 1910 the Bells went on holiday with Fry to Greece and Turkey. Vanessa had a miscarriage and was nursed by Fry – as a result they started an affair. This was succeeded by another, and much longer-lasting affair with the otherwise openly homosexual Duncan Grant (*see p.44*), a painter who she had first met soon after her marriage, when he was studying in Paris, and who became an intimate part of the Bloomsbury circle when he returned to London.

Grant was a conscientious objector, and in 1916 he and Vanessa, together with Vanessa's sons and Grant's lover David Garnett, moved to Charleston, near Firle in Sussex, so that he could escape conscription by doing agricultural labour. Charleston then became the country headquarters of the Bloomsbury Group, and Vanessa lived there from 1939 until her death. She had a daughter, Angelica, by Duncan Grant in

1918, but for many years they maintained the pretence that she was her husband's child, not that of her lover.

Vanessa had the reputation with outsiders of being somewhat difficult and antisocial, but her intimates never found her so. Leonard Woolf (*see p. 87*), who married her sister Virginia, wrote:

> *To many people she appeared frightening and formidable... I myself never found her formidable, partly because she had the most beautiful speaking voice I have ever heard, partly because of her tranquility and quietude. (The tranquility was to some extent superficial; it did not extend deep down in her mind, for there in the depths there was also an extreme sensitivity, a nervous tension...)*

Writing to Vanessa after their affair had come to an end, Roger Fry said:

> *Oh, why do I admire you so?... I think you go straight for the things that are worthwhile — you have done such an extraordinary difficult thing without any fuss; cut thro' all the conventions, kept friends with a persnickety creature like Clive, got rid of me yet kept me your devoted friend, got all the things you needed for your own development and yet managed to be a splendid mother — no, you really can't wonder. You give one a sense of security, of something solid and real in a shifting world.*

Her son Quentin remembered both her emotional depths and her sense of humour:

> *My elder brother, speaking with unconscious prescience, likened her to Demeter, a goddess who with terrible velocity could change from summer to winter. My earliest memories are of her summer laughter, specifically of an evening seated on a bench in Gordon Square when she told us how children were made and born, an account which she made so overwhelmingly droll that I rolled helpless with mirth off the bench.*

In her lifetime, Vanessa's reputation as a painter was somewhat over-shadowed by that of Grant. In hindsight, she now seems the stronger and more radical talent of the two, especially in her early paintings made just before and during World War I. Her work, like his, tended to become more conventional as she grew older.

HILAIRE BELLOC
1 8 7 0 - 1 9 5 3

SHIPLEY

A t the beginning of the 19th century, Englishmen (and of course Englishwomen) were not much troubled by the problem of 'Englishness' – that is to say, by the problem of defining who and what they were in relation to other nationalities and other regions of the world. This problem only began to trouble them as the British Empire grew. In the early years of the 20th century, after the Boer war and before the outbreak of World War I, it had become a more or less constant preoccupation. Two of the great proponents of this search were Rudyard Kipling (*see p.58*) and Hilaire Belloc. This was the more para-doxical because both of them were born abroad – Kipling in Bombay, India, Belloc in St Cloud, near Paris. Belloc's father was French, and he only became a naturalized British subject in 1902. His mother, however, was English, a granddaughter of Joseph Priestley, who was hounded out of Birmingham for his radical religious and political beliefs, and who later founded the first Unitarian church in the United States. A greater contrast to Belloc's bellicose Catholic High Toryism it would be difficult to imagine. Yet his English mother was also the source of the Catholicism that was the centre of his life. She was converted by Cardinal Manning.

Belloc was educated in England, but, since he was still a French citizen, he did his obligatory military service in France, serving with an artillery regiment near Toul in 1891. As a young man, he travelled widely, often on foot, wandering through large parts of the United States. He had always been a brilliant orator, and, for a while, when he was in his 30s, he was directly involved in politics, serving as a member of parlia-ment for South Salford in Lancashire from 1906 to 1910, sitting first as a member of the Liberal party, in a seat that had never previously elected a Liberal, then as an Independent. It was at this time that he decided to settle in Sussex, buying King's Land, in the village of Shipley, near

Horsham in 1906. His choice was significant – the Britain Belloc celebrated was even then a rural utopia, not the country created by the Industrial Revolution, which one senses he would have liked to abolish. After his time in parliament, which left him thoroughly disillusioned with political mechanisms, Belloc made a living, often precariously, as a freelance writer. He wrote on many subjects in prose and verse – producing novels, historical biographies and political tracts. No sooner had he settled in Sussex, than he produced a full-length book about it.

His best-remembered celebrations of country, however, are in verse:

> *When I am living in the Midlands*
> *That are sodden and unkind,*
> *I light my lamp in the evening:*
> *My work is left behind;*
> *And the great hills of the South Country*
> *Come back into my mind.*
>
> *The great hills of the South Country*
> *They stand along the sea;*
> *And it's there walking in the high woods*
> *That I could wish to be,*
> *And the men that were boys when I was a boy*
> *Walking along with me…*

Belloc's Top Works
- *Cautionary Tales for Children, 1896*
- *The Path to Rome, 1902*
- *Hills and the Sea, 1906*

E.F. BENSON
1867-1940

RYE

Henry James's successor at Lamb House in Rye was the prolific novelist and short story-writer Edward Frederic Benson, who moved into part of the building shortly after James died in 1916, and took over the full lease in 1920. Benson was a son of an Archbishop of Canterbury, and for part of his time in Rye he shared his home with his brother, A.C. Benson (*1862-1925*), now remembered chiefly as the author of the words that were fitted to Elgar's *Pomp and Circumstance No. 1* to create the patriotic anthem 'Land of Hope and Glory'. A.C. Benson undertook the job at the personal request of King Edward VII, shortly after the latter's accession to the throne. E.F. Benson was to be the author of a popular series of royal biographies, as well as of well-regarded ghost stories, books of memoirs and a whole series of other works – about 100 titles in all.

However, his reputation, revived by a successful television series in the 1980s, now rests on his series of comic novels about the rival ladies Mapp and Lucia. When first introduced, the two appear in quite separate narratives, though Mapp is already settled in Rye (which Benson called Tilling) in *Miss Mapp*, first published in 1922. The two did not confront one another until the publication of *Mapp & Lucia* in 1931. Two sequels followed – *Lucia's Progress* (*1935*) and *Trouble for Lucia* (*1939*) – before Benson's death in 1940. In describing Lucia's adventures he drew heavily on his own experiences in Rye, even promoting her to mayor of the town, an office he himself held for three terms.

Although Benson is a minor writer compared to his predecessor at Lamb House, he was much more intimately connected with the life of Sussex, and the social rivalries described in the Mapp and Lucia books still ring true today. Proof of the pleasure people still take in his books has been the recent appearance of two Mapp and Lucia sequels, *Lucia in Wartime* (1985) and *Lucia Triumphant* (1986). These are have been written by Tom Holt, otherwise best known as a writer of science fiction. There are also two societies, the E.F. Benson Society and the Tilling Society devoted to studying and celebrating his work.

Benson does not appear often in standard dictionaries of quotations, yet a number of his formulations have a distinctly Wildean ring. This, for example, is his description of one of his two main protagonists:

> *Though [Lucia was] essentially autocratic, her subjects were allowed and even encouraged to develop their own minds on their own lines, provided always that those lines met at the junction where she was stationmaster.*

This lies somewhere between the wit of Wilde himself and the writings of P.G. Wodehouse.

Benson's Top Works
- *Queen Lucia, 1920*
- *Miss Mapp, 1922*
- *Mapp and Lucia, 1931*

Blake's Top Works (see next page)
- *Songs of Innocence, 1789*
- *Songs of Experience, 1794*
- *The Marriage of Heaven and Hell, 1790*
- *Milton, 1803-8*

WILLIAM BLAKE
1 7 5 7 - 1 8 2 7

FELPHAM

B orn in London, the son of a prosperous hosier, William Blake lived there for most of his life. Largely educated by his mother, he began to have visionary experiences very early. In 1767, he was sent to learn drawing, which gave him the means of expressing these experiences in images as well as in words, and at the age of 14 he was apprenticed to the successful engraver, James Basire. This not only gave him an additional range of skills but introduced him to Gothic art and architecture, whose visionary qualities he immediately recognized. His mature artistic style combines Gothic elements with others taken from the then dominant Neo-classicism.

Blake's first book of poems, *Poetical Sketches*, appeared in 1783, and this was followed by many other publications, most of them both illustrated and published by himself. Meanwhile he struggled to make a living as a professional engraver and illustrator, in a highly competitive field. When, in 1800, he was invited to come and live and work in Sussex by William Hayley, a poet much richer and much better known than himself, this must have seemed like a solution to many problems.

Hayley (*1745-1820*) had an estate at Felpham. He was immensely successful in his own time – his poem *The Triumphs of Temper*, published in 1781, ran through more than a dozen editions, and its author was offered the Poet Laureateship in 1790, on the death of one of the least distinguished occupants of the post, Thomas Warton. Hayley wisely refused. He was, however, already going out of favour by the beginning of the next century – Byron later ridiculed him in *English Bards and Scotch Reviewers* (*1809*). He is now remembered for his connections to other writers – William Cowper, whose biography he wrote, and Blake.

Blake was valued by Hayley, not as a writer, but as an artist who could serve his own projects. He was Hayley's increasingly discontented guest at Felpham for three years. He was commissioned to decorate Hayley's library with 18 portraits of poets – one of these was a portrait of Milton, now in Manchester City Art Gallery – and to make illustrations for the projected *Life of Cowper*. In addition he had to provide illustrations for Hayley's own insipid writings – among them a ballad, *Little Tom the Sailor*, and a further series of *Ballads Based on Anecdotes Relating to Animals*.

Blake liked Felpham at first – soon after his arrival there he wrote to his friend Thomas Butts to describe his new situation:

> *We are safe arrived at our cottage without accident or hindrance. We had seven different chaises and as many different drivers. We travelled through a most beautiful country on a most glorious day. Our cottage is beautiful. If I should ever build a palace it would be only my cottage enlarged. The villagers of Felpham are polite and modest. Meat is cheaper than in London. The sweet air and voices of winds, trees and birds, and the odors of the happy ground, makes it a dwelling for immortals.*

This sunny mood did not last – Blake soon grew fed up with the tasks Hayley imposed on him, which tended to interrupt his own visionary broodings. He was then starting work on *Milton* (published in 1803, soon after he left Sussex) and on 'Jerusalem'. Matters came to a head when he tried to drive a drunken soldier called John Scolfield out of his cottage garden. The Napoleonic Wars were at their height, and Scolfield laid evidence against him as a possible subversive:

> *Blake said the French knew our strength very well, and if the French set foot on English ground that every Englishman would be put to his choice whether to have his throat cut or to join the French and that he was a strong man and would certainly begin to cut throats and the strongest man must conquer – that he damned the King of England – his country and his subjects – that his soldiers were all bound for slaves and all the poor people in general.*

Blake returned to town, but was charged with high treason and tried at Chichester Assizes in 1804. He was easily acquitted. His experience at Felpham cured him of any taste for the countryside. Afterwards he told Butts that it was only possible to have visions in London.

SIR DIRK BOGARDE
1921-1999

ALFRISTON

Dirk Bogarde, born Derek van den Bogaerde in Hampstead of mixed Belgian and Scottish ancestry, is best remembered for his career as an actor. Starting out as a matinée idol in the 1950s (on his death Glenda Jackson described him as the Leonardo di Caprio of the period), when he made his name as the handsome young Simon Sparrow, hero of the 'Doctor' series, he went on to star in difficult, complex films by major directors, among them Joseph Losey's *The Servant* (*1963*) and Luchino Visconti's *The Damned* (*1969*) and *Death in Venice* (*1971*). During the latter years of his success as an actor, Bogarde lived mostly in Provence with his partner Tony Forwood, moving back to London in 1988 when Forwood fell ill with cancer. Forwood's importance in Bogarde's life was only full acknowledged after his death. Neither of them seems to have thought of moving to Sussex. However, Bogarde claims a place in this book because his Sussex childhood played an important role in his books – he wrote both a series of memoirs and novels that are often obviously based on his own life.

Bogarde was brought up at Lullington, near Alfriston, in Sussex not by his parents (his father was the first art editor of *The Times*), but by his older sister Elizabeth and their adored nurse Lally. The county figures in his first volume of memoirs, *A Postillion Struck by Lightning*, published in 1977, and also, more intensely in the novel-memoir *Great Meadow* (*1992*), which recalls his intense response to nature as an 11-year-old boy, and again, more obliquely in his final novel, *Closing Ranks* (*1997*). One curious feature of this last book is that, while it tells the story of an upper-class family gathered round the death-bed of a beloved nanny, the dying woman curses them instead of blessing them.

In fact Bogarde seems to have felt a real ambivalence both about his family and about Sussex. It only emerged, some three years after his death, that he had a long-lost paternal grandfather who had lived in Brighton, reappearing there many years after deserting his wife and son. Aimé van den Bogaerde was an adventurer who, having lost all his money, sailed for Colombia in 1899, to try his luck as an orchid hunter. At first he sent optimistic reports of his progress but, soon after announcing his intention to return home with his fortunes restored, he ceased to communicate with his family. His wife died in 1917, believing he had been killed in South America.

When Aimé reappeared in 1931, his son Ulric, resenting his behaviour, refused to have anything to do with him, but Dirk, who had some contact with him, was apparently fascinated, although Aimé does not figure in any of his books of reminiscences. The returned prodigal, who died in 1938, was an alcoholic who forged paintings for a living, or else touted his own art round the pubs of Brighton in exchange for drink. He sounds very much like the kind of flawed character that Bogarde might have played in the later years of his film career.

Bogarde's Top Works

❯ *A Postillion Struck by Lightning, 1977*

❯ *Voices in the Garden, 1981*

❯ *A Short Walk from Harrods, 1993*

Brangwyn's Top Works (see next page)

❯ *The Return of the Fishing Fleet, 1888*

❯ *A Cooper at Work, 1905*

❯ *British Empire Panels, 1924-33*

SIR FRANK BRANGWYN
1867-1956

DITCHLING

Frank Brangwyn was born in Bruges, the son of an English father and a Welsh mother. His father was involved with church decoration, which gave his son some artistic background, but as an artist he was largely self-taught. The family returned to live in London in 1874 and, in 1882, through his father's contacts with the Arts and Crafts movement, Brangwyn was introduced to William Morris, who took him on as apprentice. He remained with Morris for two years, but soon became restless and wanted to establish his own artistic independence. A turning point was reached in 1885 when, aged only 17, he had a painting accepted for the Royal Academy Summer Exhibition.

Brangwyn travelled widely as soon as he could afford to do so, making expeditions to Belgium, Central Europe, South Africa, Spain and Morocco. He established a reputation as an immensely prolific illustrator as well as a painter. Unlike most of his British contemporaries he swiftly became well-known abroad. In 1893 he was invited to become a corresponding member of the Munich Secession; in 1895 one of his paintings was purchased by the French government, and in the same year the Paris dealer Samuel Bing commissioned Brangwyn to paint murals for the façade of his shop La Maison de l'Art Nouveau in Paris. This emporium was the cradle of the Europe-wide Art Nouveau movement, which seemed to represent everything innovative in art in the closing years of the 19th century. In 1898 he was awarded a Gold Medal at the Munich International Art Exhibition and in 1902 he was given the Legion of Honour.

Until 1917 Brangwyn continued to live and work in London. Then he and his wife Lucy moved to Ditchling in Sussex, in order to escape from the Zeppelin raids on London. They bought a house called The Jointure in Ditchling the following year.

World War I and the move to Ditchling represented a turning point in Brangwyn's fortunes as an artist. His reputation in England, slower to grow than on the continent of Europe, was apparently confirmed by his election as a full member of the Royal Academy in 1919. (He had been an ARA in 1904, so his acceptance there was rather belated.) At the same time, however, he started to drift slowly out of fashion.

In 1924 his wife died, and he became increasingly reluctant to travel, despite the major decorative commissions that were now coming his way. The most important of these was for a series of panels for the Royal Gallery of the House of Lords, commemorating World War I. The first paintings Brangwyn produced were considered too gloomy, and he began again, with others that celebrated 'the peoples and produce of the great Empire'. By 1927 five out of a planned 16 panels had been completed. They were shown to a House of Lords committee, which, prompted by the negative reaction of the Royal Commission of Fine Art, turned them down as too rich and exotic for the intended setting. What this implied, in coded terms, was that the celebration of the whole Imperial idea, with which Brangwyn had long been associated, was becoming an embarrassment in post-war circumstances. The series was eventually completed in 1933, and found a home in Swansea Guildhall.

Brangwyn's flame flickered on for a while. In the early 1930s, he painted murals for the Rockefeller Center in New York, receiving less kudos though also stirring up less trouble than Diego Rivera, who worked there at the same period. He designed and decorated a series of sumptuous dining saloons for the Canadian Pacific liner *Empress of Britain*, torpedoed in World War II, and was knighted in 1941, although he never collected the honour. A brief visit to Chipping Campden in the same year was the last time he set foot outside Ditchling.

Though the Royal Academy gave him at major retrospective in 1952 – the first occasion it had staged such an exhibition for a living artist – Brangwyn was rapidly forgotten after his death in 1956. He was not a Modernist, and at the same time he did not fit comfortably into the history of Victorian and post-Victorian academic art. His reputation has only recently begun to revive.

SIR EDWARD BURNE-JONES
1 8 3 3 - 1 8 9 8

ROTTINGDEAN

Fans of the Pre-Raphaelites movement are often a little surprised to discover that Edward Burne-Jones's ashes are buried at Rottingdean. In geographical terms, he is associated with Birmingham, where he was born, with Oxford, where he met his close friend and professional associate William Morris, and with London, where he lived for many years at The Grange in West Kensington. The Grange was then an old farmhouse that was gradually being swallowed up by urban London, pushing westwards from Kensington proper. Where it once stood, there is now a bunch of council flats.

Rottingdean was where Burne-Jones had a holiday home – North End House – a large house formed by throwing together three existing buildings, including Prospect Cottage and Aubrey House It formed a headquarters for his extended family, or, rather, for the extended family of his wife Georgie, who managed his life for him. Georgie, born Macdonald, was one of four remarkable sisters. One married the successful academic painter Sir Edward Poynter. Another became the mother of Rudyard Kipling (*see p. 58*). The fourth, who was married to a headmaster, was the mother of Stanley Baldwin, Conservative Prime Minister from 1923-9 and from 1935-7.

Burne-Jones made his success only gradually – paradoxically, when it came, it was partly generated by his reluctance to exhibit publicly, preferring to depend on a small elite of wealthy and sophisticated patrons. It was not until he exhibited at the newly founded Grosvenor Gallery in 1877 that he became nationally famous. By the 1880s he was regarded at home as Britain's greatest living artist. In 1889 he was awarded a Gold

Medal at the Exhibition Universelle in Paris, which established his reputation firmly abroad. His work had an impact in surprising places – for example, it can be detected in some of the paintings of Picasso's Blue Period. But his enclosed poetic universe was affected not at all by what surrounded him in Sussex. His importance there was that, through his wife and not through any effort of his own, he made it into a place that was known to artists and intellectuals. Without the Burne-Jones connection to attract him, Kipling would never have chosen to settle in Sussex.

Burne-Jones's Top Works

- *Stained glass at Christ Church Cathedral, Oxford, 1870s*
- *The Wheel of Fortune, 1875-83*
- *East Window at St Margaret's, Rottingdean, 1893*

SIR ARTHUR CONAN DOYLE
1859-1930

CROWBOROUGH

Arthur Ignatius Conan Doyle was born in Edinburgh, but came from Irish Catholic stock. He was educated at Stonyhurst, the great English Catholic boarding school, which he hated, then returned to Edinburgh to study medicine. During his student years he began to write fiction in his spare time. After adventurous voyages to the Arctic (which fascinated him) and Africa (which he disliked), he set up an independent medical practice in Portsmouth. In 1885 he married, and in 1888 he published his first Sherlock Holmes novel, *A Study in Scarlet*. This was followed two years later by another, *The Sign of Four*, featuring the same hero, which made Conan Doyle famous on both sides of the Atlantic. Holmes was to haunt his creator for the rest of his life, as Conan Doyle tended to prefer his other, more 'serious' writings, such as the historical novel *The White Company*. By 1893 he had already decided to get rid of his burdensome hero, and wrote a story called *The Final Problem*, in which Holmes and his inveterate enemy Professor Moriarty fall to their deaths at the Reichenbach Falls in Switzerland. However, this absence did not last, as Holmes was already well on his way to becoming a national icon – a position he still occupies today.

The health of Conan Doyle's wife Louisa was now in terminal decline from tuberculosis, and he was in love with Jean Leckie, who was to become his adored second wife. In 1900 he volunteered for service as a doctor during the Boer War, and wrote an account of his experiences that earned him a knighthood in 1902 (it may also have helped that Edward VII was a great fan of Sherlock Holmes). He revived Holmes in 1901, with one of his most celebrated books, *The Hound of the Baskervilles*, where the detective moves in the realm of the uncanny, which was to become an obsessive interest in his creator's later years.

In 1906 his wife died, and in 1907 he was at long last able to marry Jean. It was at this point that he moved to Sussex – his second wife's family came from the county. In the year of his marriage he bought an old house called Windlesham near Crowborough, to which he made substantial additions. He lived there for the rest of his life, though he also kept a small flat in London.

Sussex makes a number of appearances in Conan Doyle's later fictions. Holmes, having moved from London, is imagined spending his retirement as a Sussex bee-keeper, in *The Sussex Vampire*, one of Conan Doyle's last set of Sherlock Holmes stories. Published in 1924, it contains a detailed description of what is probably the author's own house, now set near a fictional town named Lamberley. Here is Holmes's and Watson's first glimpse of it:

> It was evening of a dull, foggy November day when, having left our bags at the Chequers, Lamberley, we drove through the Sussex clay of a long winding lane and finally reached the isolated and ancient farmhouse in which Ferguson dwelt. It was a large, straggling building, very old in the centre, very new at the wings with towering Tudor chimneys and a lichen-spotted, high-pitched roof of Horsham slabs. The doorsteps were worn into curves, and the ancient tiles which lined the porch were marked with the rebus of a cheese and a man after the original builder.

Conan Doyle fitted comfortably into the kind of mental space occupied by his contemporaries Kipling (*see p. 58*) and Belloc (*see p. 20*). He and Kipling were friends, despite the latter's increasing reclusiveness, and used to play golf together. As with Kipling, Conan Doyle's temperament had a mystical side, which became more pronounced as he grew older. In later life he became a strong supporter of Spiritualism, and devoted much time and money to the cause.

Conan Doyle's Top Works
- *A Study in Scarlet, 1888*
- *The Adventures of Sherlock Holmes, 1891*
- *The Hound of the Baskervilles, 1901*

JOHN CONSTABLE
1776-1837

BRIGHTON

B orn in 1776, in East Bergholt, Suffolk, Constable was the son of a prosperous corn merchant. When he began to study art, after a long struggle against his father's prejudices, he entered the Royal Academy schools in London in 1799. While annual exhibitions at the Academy became the arena in which he struggled for success, often seeming to make little headway against the much more celebrated J.M.W. Turner (*see p.82*), he retained deep roots in his native Suffolk, and most of his major compositions are depictions of the Suffolk landscape. Sussex, and particularly Brighton do not immediately spring to mind in connection with him. Yet one of his most ambitious late compositions is an image of Brighton beach. Constable first visited the town in 1824, going there for the sake of the health of his wife Maria. At first he hated it. He wrote to his friend Archdeacon John Fisher:

> *Brighton is the receptacle of the fashion and off-scouring of London. The magnifence of the sea and its ... everlasting voice is drowned in the dun & lost in the tumut of stage coaches, gigs; flys' &c. — and the beach is only Piccadilly by the sea-side. Ladies dressed & undressed — Gentlemen in morning gowns & slippers on, or without them altogether about knee-deep in the breakers — footmen — children — nursery maids, dogs, boys, fishermen — preventive service men [i.e. customs officials] (with hangers and pistols) rotten fish & those hideous amphibious animals the old bathing women, whose language both in oaths & voice resembles men — are all mixed together in endless indecent confusion. The genteeler part, the marine parade, is still more unnatural — with its trimmed and neat appearance & the dandy jetty or chain pier, with its long and elegant strides into the sea a full 1/4 mile. In short there is nothing here for a painter but the breakers — & sky — which have been lovely indeed... The fishing boats are picturesque.*

However his hostile feelings about Brighton gradually softened, and by 1826 he was thinking of making a large painting using a Brighton theme. The project gradually evolved into one of his 'six-footers', the most ambitious canvases he ever made, things on which he hoped his reputation with posterity would rest. The finished result was shown in the Royal Academy's annual exhibition of 1827. The painting features the chain pier and, half-concealed behind the sails of a fishing boat, the newly completed Albion Hotel. On the beach, in addition to figures representative of Brighton's traditional fishing industry, are representatives of the fashionable visitors who now came to Brighton. In the very centre of the composition, for example, are two fashionably dressed women with parasols, trying to make headway against the wind. These are the forerunners of the elegant ladies who appear some years later in Eugène Boudin's paintings of the beach at Deauville. As the authors of the catalogue of a recent Tate Britain exhibition devoted to Constable remarked:

> In the Chain Pier…Constable creates a memorable portrait of a coastal town at a key moment of historical transition.

~~~

Constable's Top Works
- *The Hay Wain, 1821*
- *Chain Pier, 1826-7*
- *Arundel Mill and Castle, 1837*

ELIZABETH DAVID
1913-1992

FOLKINGTON

The career of Elizabeth David, Britain's most revolutionary writer on cookery, can be thought of as a life-long rebellion against her upper-class Sussex background. She grew up at Wootton Manor, a 17th-century Sussex country house. Her father, Rupert Gwynne, was Tory MP for Eastbourne; her mother was the Honourable Stella Ridley, daughter of the 1st Viscount Ridley, who had been Home Secretary from 1895 to 1900, in Lord Salisbury's second administration. Her father died in 1924, and in 1933 her mother married John Hamillton.

David's first escape from this impeccably Conservative – in all senses of the word – background, with its dull food, was when she was sent to learn French at the Sorbonne at the age of 19. Not long after, she left home, with ambitions to be an actress. By 1939 she had a married lover, Charles Gibson Cowan, with whom she bought a boat – their ambition was to sail round the Mediterranean together. They were caught in France by the outbreak of war, the occupying Germans impounded their craft in Antibes, and together they fled to Syros in the Cyclades, an island that offers somewhat better than average Greek food. When the Germans invaded Greece, they fled again to Cairo. Here the couple split up, and David began working for the Ministry of Information. She also decided that it would be more convenient to be married – to Lieutenant-Colonel Tony David. About this union she was always lukewarm, though she retained her husband's surname.

When she returned to England she was shocked by the dullness as well as the austerity of the British post-war diet. She started writing articles about cookery in 1946, and in 1950 published a book,

Mediterranean Food, which started an enormous change in attitudes to diet. It introduced her readers to ingredients, such as aubergines, courgettes and saffron, that were hitherto unknown to most of them. At this time even olive oil was scarcely known as an ingredient for cooking, but was bought instead from chemist shops as a recipe for earache.

Mediterranean Food was followed by a number of other extremely influential cookbooks – *French Country Cooking* (1951), *Italian Food* (1954), *Summer Cooking* (1955), *French Provincial Cooking* (1961). In 1965, David started a cookery shop in Pimlico, to sell the pots and other implements she preferred, sourced from their countries of origin.

In 1969, aged 56, she suffered a stroke, perhaps caused by her heavy drinking. This deprived her of the ability to taste salt, and also curbed her enthusiasm for taking lovers. She nevertheless continued to be influential as a preacher, researcher and theoretician about food, and continues to be so now, almost a decade and a half after her death. She possessed an unrivalled ability not only to construct practical and usable recipes, but to connect these with the sensual pleasures of travel abroad, to warmer and more colourful lands.

David's Top Works
- *Mediterranean Cooking, 1950*
- *French Country Cooking, 1951*
- *An Omelette and a Glass of Wine, 1984*

CHRISTOPHER FRY
1907-2005

COLEMAN'S HATCH

The playwright Christopher Fry was born Christopher Harris in Bristol and brought up in Bedford. He took his maternal grand-mother's name because he had Quaker sympathies, and thought – mistakenly – that she had a link to the great Quaker family. He began writing at the age of 11, and by the time he was 14 he had already produced a full-length verse-play.

In his youth, he worked as a prep-school master, then as a travelling organizer for Dr Barnado's Homes. By 1932 he was already involved with the professional theatre. In that year he was a founder member of the Tunbridge Wells Repertory Players, directing the English premiere of George Bernard Shaw's *A Village Wooing* in 1934.

In 1936, he married and moved to Coleman's Hatch in Sussex. Here the vicar of the local church, Holy Trinity, asked him to write a play for the church's jubilee. The result was *Boy with a Cart (1938)*, which told the story of the early Sussex saint, St Cuthman, who pushed his crippled mother in a wheelbarrow all the way from Cornwall to Steyning in Sussex. This commission brought Fry into touch with the religious drama movement, featuring plays in verse, which was just starting to blossom at that time under the leadership of T. S. Eliot, whose play *Murder in the Cathedral* appeared in 1935.

Fry and Eliot were soon in touch. When World War II broke out in 1939, Fry, though by instinct a conscientious objector, realised that he must play his part. Eliot suggested that he join the London Fire Service, but Fry objected that he had no head for heights. 'Then you must special-ize in basements', the great man said. In the event, Fry joined the pioneer corps, fighting fires in the Liverpool docks.

Fry's moment of success began immediately after the war, with the one-act comedy *A Phoenix Too Frequent*, presented at the Mercury Theatre in London in 1946. On the strength of this, he was appointed staff dramatist at the Arts Theatre, and after some travail found a subject in a novella entitled *Wooing the Gallows*, by the German writer Wilhelm Heinrich von Riehl (*1823-1897*) – a retelling of a medieval folk-tale. The result was his most successful play, *The Lady's Not for Burning* (*1948*).

Fry was a huge success for the next four or five years, to the point where *The Observer*'s then theatre critic, Ivor Brown, commented that 'Our theatre is now beginning to consist of Large Fry and Small Fry'.

Soon enough, however, the public started to tire of Fry's glittering cascades of words, and at the same time Fry found that his inspiration had begun to flag. He turned to making translations and adaptations, and to writing scripts, sometimes uncredited, for films and television. One film to which he made a major uncredited contribution was William Wyler's epic *Ben Hur* (*1959*), starring Charlton Heston. Fry spent 14 months in Rome, rewriting practically all of the original script.

Fry was never embittered by the fact that his work had abruptly gone out of fashion. In his years of semi-obscurity he maintained cordial links with his local theatre in Chichester. His translations of Ibsen's *Peer Gynt* and Rostands's *Cyrano de Bergerac* were produced there in the 1970s. In 1992 Chichester saw a revival of *Venus Observed* (*1959*), originally written for Laurence Olivier, and one of *The Lady's Not for Burning* in 2002.

Fry's Top Works
- *A Phoenix too Frequent, 1946*
- *The Lady's Not for Burning, 1948*
- *Venus Observ'd, 1949*

STELLA GIBBONS
1902 - 1989

'HOWLING'

Stella Gibbons was born in London, the daughter of a doctor, and became famous for one novel, her first, *Cold Comfort Farm*, published in 1932. Though not written in Sussex, it offers a delicious, unforgettably comic fantasy about rural life in the remoter parts of the county. It offers a rustic counterpart to E.F. Benson's comedies about Sussex small-town life, which belong to the same epoch, but is a good deal sharper in tone.

Gibbons was provoked into writing the book when she was asked by the *Evening Standard*, the newspaper for which she then worked, to write a précis of *The Golden Arrow* (written in 1916), an over-heated rural novel by Mary Webb, who had just become posthumously famous thanks to the success of a later book of the same sort, *Precious Bane (1924)*.

As Gibbons's nephew and biographer Reggie Olivier notes, in a website devoted to his aunt,

> Stella began to wonder how the grim, outlandish characters of Webb's
> suffocating rural milieu might fare if confronted by a brisk, smart, sensible
> young lady from London.

Mary Webb's novels were set in Shropshire, and the name 'Cold Comfort Farm', suggested by a friend, derived from a real place of that name near Hinckley in Leicestershire. Gibbons nevertheless decided to set her story in Sussex, in the fictional village of Howling. One reason for this may have been that Sussex represented a kind of rural idyll more directly accessible, in the physical sense, to Londoners such as her briskly commonsensical heroine Flora Poste. Another reason may have been that Gibbons found a useful secondary source in the equally glum rural novels of Sheila Kaye-Smith, which were in fact set in the county. Kaye-Smith, a lesbian and a Catholic convert married to an Anglo-Catholic clergyman (she was also, rather improbably, a friend of Noel Coward) had made her reputation with a novel called *Sussex Gorse*, published in 1916 and reprinted many times subsequently. Its chief character, Reuben Backfield, is like Gibbons's Reuben Starkadder, obsessed with the desire to possess a particular piece of rural property.

One of the delights of *Cold Comfort Farm* is its inventiveness with language. Where her model, Mary Webb, used genuine fragments of rural dialect in an attempt to give her work authenticity, Gibbons blithely invented the terms she needed. Some, such as 'mollocking' and 'suke-bind' – both with erotic implications – have entered the mainstream of the language.

Cold Comfort Farm won Gibbons a prestigious literary prize, the Prix Femina Vie-Heureuse for 1933. Ironically enough, this prize had also been won by Mary Webb's *Precious Bane*, only a few years previously. The award to Gibbons greatly irritated Virginia Woolf, of whom more will be said later in this book – Woolf thought it should have gone to her friend Rosamund Lehmann. Another, subliminal cause of irritation may have been the gleeful parody of intense, self-dramatizing relationships, which is a major theme in *Cold Comfort Farm*. This element in the book was based on the behaviour of Gibbons's own family. Though the melo-dramatic Starkadders are in theory miles apart from the hyper-refined denizens of Bloomsbury, self-dramatization was something the two milieux undoubtedly had in common.

Gibbon's Top Works
- *Cold Comfort Farm, 1932*
- *The Match Maker, 1949*
- *Here be Dragons, 1956*

Gill's Top Works (see next page)
- *Ecstasy, 1910-11*
- *Prospero and Ariel, 1932*
- *Lovers, 1934*

ERIC GILL
1882-1940

DITCHLING

Unlike most of the artists and writers whose lives appear here, Gill was born in Sussex, in Brighton. The son of a clergyman, he spent his teenage years in Chichester, then studied lettering under the calligrapher Edward Johnson at the Central School of Arts and Crafts in London. He got married in 1906, to the daughter of the sacristan at Chichester cathedral, and a little later moved to Ditchling, living first in Ditchling Village, then moving, after his conversion to Catholicism in 1913, to Hopkin's Crank, a comfortless, unreconstructed Georgian cottage on Ditchling Common. Here he soon gathered a band of disciples around him as he pursued his ideal of a fully integrated artistic life – as he put it,

> *Life and work and love and the bringing up of a family and clothes and social virtues and food and houses and games and songs and books should all be in the soup together.*

In 1914 Gill produced the series of sculptures that helped to make him nationally famous – the Stations of the Cross in Westminster Cathedral. These are clearly influenced by the famous Norman reliefs in Chichester cathedral, with which he had been familiar since his childhood. After World War I he tried to make a more regular framework for his artistic and domestic ideals by founding the Guild of St Joseph and St Dominic at Ditchling. David Jones (*see p. 56*) was a member and one of his pupils.

In 1924 Gill suddenly decided to uproot himself from Sussex, moving with his whole entourage to the ruined Benedictine monastery of Capell-y-ffin in the Black Mountains of Wales. It was during his time in Wales that Gill created the Monotype type-face Gill Sans that has been his enduring legacy to Modernist typography. It represents an unexpected reconciliation to the world of the machine, which till then he had violently rejected. In 1928, he moved again, to Pigotts, near High Wycombe in Buckinghamshire, where he set up a printing press.

His later years were filled with important commissions, among them the sculpture of Prospero and Ariel for Broadcasting House in London and three reliefs for the League of Nations headquarters in Geneva. Gill was made a Royal Designer for Industry by the Royal Society of Arts and became a founder-member of the newly established Faculty of Royal Designers for Industry. All of these were signs of his acceptance, despite his apparently eccentric background, by the British establishment. He died at Uxbridge, Middlesex, in 1940.

In 1989, nearly 50 years after his death, a revelatory light was cast on Gill's private life and personality by a new biography written by Fiona MacCarthy, based on Gill's meticulous diaries, now lodged with the University of California. Her book revealed, among other things, that Gill had been regularly unfaithful to his wife, that he had had incestuous relationships with his two elder daughters, and that he had even (in his time at Pigotts) indulged in bestiality with the family dog.

These revelations caused uproar amongst some of the more devout of Gill's admirers. The Catholic Mothers' Union demanded that his Stations be banished from Westminster, and nearly succeeded in getting their way, only foiled by its status as a Listed Building. Yet the fuss was in one sense surprising, since Gill was already known for the number of erotic works he had produced, side by side with his religious ones – during his Ditchling years he made an almost-life-size sculpture of his sister Gladys and her husband copulating, which he called simply *Fucking*. However, when this passed into the possession of the Tate Gallery, having been found abandoned in a boathouse in Birchington-on-Sea, it was prudently re-titled *Ecstacy*. Perhaps partly as a result of the controversy, there is a lively interest in Gill's life and work today. His achievement covers a wide variety of different activities – in addition to being a sculptor, typographer and maker of monumental inscriptions, he was a prolific maker of beautiful prints that are closely related to his carvings.

DUNCAN GRANT
1885-1978

CHARLESTON

Duncan Grant was born in Inverness, and spent part of his childhood in India and Burma, where his father was serving as an army officer. He was sent home in 1894 to attend St Paul's School in London. When he was 17, since he seemed a hopeless prospect for the army, which was the career his father had intended for him, it was decided that he would go to Westminster School of Art and live with Sir Richard and Lady Strachey, the parents of his cousin, the writer Lytton Strachey, five years older than himself. Despite initial resistance from Grant – 'Relations we may be,' he said, 'have them we may not.' – Lytton became the first of Grant's many male lovers.

In 1906 Grant went to Paris to continue his studies, with a letter of introduction to the French painter Simon Bussy, who was married to Dorothy Strachey, Lytton's sister. Bussy was a friend of Matisse, but the excitements of the emergent Fauve movement seem at that point to have passed Grant by. He studied at the new art school set up by the fashionable portrait painter Jacques-Emile Blanche, who was also a perspicacious critic, and copied the Old Masters in the Louvre.

On his return from Paris Grant entered into an even closer relation-ship with the Bloomsbury Group than that already fostered by his link with the Stracheys. In 1908 he began an affair with the brilliant econo-mist and connoisseur of art John Maynard Keynes, who was part of the Bloomsbury connection with Cambridge University (Lytton Strachey had been Keynes's close friend and fellow student there), and travelled widely with him in Europe. He learned about Picasso, Matisse and Derain. In 1910 Grant met Roger Fry, and became a co-director of the Omega Workshops, which Fry founded in 1913.

When World War I broke out, Grant and his new lover, the writer David Garnett, were conscientious objectors. They worked first as farm-labourers in Suffolk, then moved in 1916 to Charleston, near Firle, to set up a household with Vanessa Bell (*see p.18*) and her two children. Grant was to live there for most of the rest of his life.

During the 1920s, and up until the middle of the 1930s, Grant was a very fashionable artist, perhaps the best-known of all British Modernists. It certainly helped that two of the leading critics of the time, Roger Fry and Clive Bell, were cheer-leaders for his work. Despite this his first major commission, two murals for the refectory of what is now South Bank University (formerly the Borough Polytechnic Institute) painted in 1911 was condemned by the *Times* newspaper as possibly a 'degenerative influence on the children of the working class'. The two paintings now belong to the Tate. By 1936 he was sufficiently well regarded to be commissioned to create decorations for the new trans-atlantic liner *Queen Mary*, though these were in the end rejected as being too avant-garde.

It is clear that Grant had a personality of quite extraordinary charisma. In 1929 his fellow artist, Walter Sickert, said of him, 'Duncan Grant, like another gentleman in Europe in a somewhat more difficult line of business, was born with a crown on his head.' Sickert was referring to Alfonso XIII, then King of Spain. 'Duncan conquered', Sickert added, 'he saw, he came.' Vanessa Bell, writing, to her son Julian in 1937, said:

> He is so incredibly full of charm, his genius as an artist seems to overflow so into his life and character & he is so amusing too and odd and unaccountable that lots of people I think don't see clearly what to me is really his most adorable quality – his honesty – disinterestedness, absolute sincerity & simplicity of character which make me depend upon him always.

The trouble with this heartfelt tribute is that 'genius' now seems the wrong word. Grant was a painter of abundant talent, but it was a talent that was never quite focused and never quite fulfilled itself. This is the reason that his work is half-forgotten today. The light-hearted decorations at Charleston, carried out in collaboration with Vanessa Bell, are perhaps the most attractive part of his legacy, since they speak so eloquently about the Bloomsbury lifestyle.

GRAHAM GREENE
1904-1991

BRIGHTON

Few, if indeed any, amateurs of literature would classify Graham Greene as a 'Sussex author', yet his novel *Brighton Rock*, first published in 1938, is undoubtedly one of the more striking evocations of an aspect of Sussex life. John Boulting, who directed the 1947 film based on the book (with a script by Greene and Terence Rattigan), was attracted to the book chiefly for its vivid evocation of a sense of place. 'The setting was not a backdrop,' he said, 'it was one of the characters.' Both the book and the film evoke a seedy ambience of bar rooms, racetracks, cafés and boarding houses. In 1947 it seemed like an evocation of the spiv culture that had grown up in Britain during the war, but a version of this seedy life had in fact flourished in Brighton during the late 1930s.

When the book was written Greene was already the rootless, restless world traveller he was to remain throughout his life. Brighton, as the location for his story, was unusual chiefly in the sense that it was nearer home than the exotic settings he usually preferred – Africa, Mexico, Haiti. To all of these places, he brought the same detached powers of observation.

Greene himself was typically ambiguous in his comments about his chosen *mise-en-scène* which seem to contradict the sense of authenticity that Boulting found in the book:

> ... *the setting of* Brighton Rock *may in part belong to an imaginary geographic region. Though Nelson Place has been cleared away since the war, and the Brighton race gangs were to all intents quashed forever as a serious menace at Lewes Assizes a little before the date of my novel, and even Sherry's*

dance hall has vanished, they certainly did exist; there was a real Nelson Place, and a man was kidnapped on Brighton front in a broad daylight of the thirties, though not in the same circumstances as Hale, and his body was found somewhere out towards the Downs flung from a car. Colleoni, the gang leader, had his real prototype who had retired by 1938 and lived a gracious Catholic life in one of the Brighton crescents, although I found his name was still law when I demanded entrance by virtue of it to a little London nightclub called The Nest behind Regent Street...

All the same I must plead guilty to manufacturing this Brighton of mine as I never manufactured Mexico or Indochina. There were no living models for these gangsters, nor for the barmaid who so obstinately refused to come alive. I had spent only one night in the company of someone who could have belonged to Pinkie's gang – a man from the Wandsworth dog-tracks whose face had been carved because he was suspected of grassing to the bogies after a killing in the stadium. (He taught me the only professional slang I knew, but one cannot learn a language in one night, however long.)

Yet *Brighton Rock* grips one as an imaginative creation more surely than almost any of the novels that celebrate the rural glories of Sussex. It offers a reminder that this, one of the most beautiful of all English counties also has an organic link to London that does not exist in other rural areas of the same type. It is not suburban, like large tracts of Middlesex and Essex, but London is nevertheless something that contributes largely to its identity.

Grant's Top Works (see previous page)
- ❯ *Lytton Strachey, c.1909*
- ❯ *Omega Flowers on the Mantelpiece, 46 Gordon Square, 1912*
- ❯ *Vanessa Bell, 1918*

Greene's Top Works
- ❯ *Brighton Rock, 1938*
- ❯ *The End of the Affair, 1951*
- ❯ *Travels with My Aunt, 1969*

PATRICK HAMILTON
1904-1962

BRIGHTON

The unhappy, alcoholic child of alcoholic parents, both of whom were also minor writers, Patrick Hamilton wrote two sensationally successful plays, *Rope* (*1929*) and *Gas Light* (*1938*). The first of these, apparently based on the Leopold and Loeb killing-for-kicks murder case in America (though Hamilton always denied there was a link) was made into a memorably tense film in 1948 by Alfred Hitchcock, in which the director pioneered the use of very long, apparently seamless takes. The second, a Victorian drama about a man who marries for money and then tries to drive his wife mad in order to lay hands on her fortune, was filmed twice, first in Britain (*1940*), with Diana Wynyard, then in Hollywood (*1944*). The second version, directed by George Cukor, starred Ingrid Bergman as the victim. She won a Best Actress Oscar for her performance. Neither of these dramas has anything to do with Sussex.

Brighton is, however, the setting for one of Hamilton's novels, which many people think are better than his plays. This novel, *The West Pier* (*1951*), was described by Graham Greene, who had his own taste for the sleazy, as 'the best book written about Brighton'. It forms part of a trilogy about a psychopathic young con-man called Ralph Ernest Gorse, whose character was based in part at least, on that of the role-playing double-murderer Neville Heath, hanged in 1946.

Hamilton has always evoked the admiration of other writers, in particular for his ear for dialogue. His friend Claud Cockburn said of him:

> *Just as some people can listen to a voice once and an hour later mimic it perfectly, so Hamilton could listen, without even seeming to listen, to a half-hour's conversation going on at the other end of a bar and afterwards not only reproduce its content and cadences, but intuitively deduce from it the whole nature of the talkers.*

Doris Lessing, one of his greatest fans, notes:

Never has anyone written about crooks as well as Hamilton.
And it's the details that are so absorbing.

In his descriptions of miserable, penny-pinching lives soaked in self-deception and alcohol, Hamilton remains unsurpassed. In his description of Brighton he offers a vision of Sussex life very different from most others yet intensely convincing in itself.

Hamilton's Top Works
- *20,000 Streets under the Sky, 1935*
- *Hangover Square, 1941*
- *The West Pier, 1951*

IVON HITCHENS
1893-1979

MIDHURST

Ivon Hitchens, who spent nearly 40 years living and painting in Sussex, offers proof that you don't have to live a dramatic life to be a good artist. The son of a landscape painter, he was educated at Bedale's, a progressive boarding school, then at the St John's Wood School of Art and the Royal Academy Schools. In 1922, having already made a reputation as a member of the rather tentative British avant-garde of the period, he was a founding member of the Seven and Five Society, and an associate of Ben Nicholson, Barbara Hepworth, Paul Nash and Henry Moore. He was influenced by Winifred Nicholson, Ben Nicholson's first wife, whom he met in 1925 – she was a remarkable painter whose work is still underestimated. He also fell under the spell of the work that Braque was producing between the wars and felt the seduction of Cézanne.

In 1940 the course of his life was changed when a bomb fell next door to the studio he occupied in Adelaide Road, Hampstead. A year previously he had bought a tract of land at Lavington Common near Midhurst. He and his wife now went to live on this, at first inhabiting a traditional showman's caravan. Later this was replaced by a two-storey house and adjacent studios.

Though Hitchens painted nudes, still-lifes and interiors, he was from the time that he settled in Sussex primarily a painter of landscape, using, almost exclusively, a panoramic, double-cube format that allowed him to represent sweeping vistas. These vistas were not precise representations of what surrounded him, but a semi-abstract presentation of his own feelings and sensations. His attitudes are accurately reflected in his statement:

I paint life as I see it, hear it, smell it and think it, but above all see it. It is sifted through one's intelligence. The canvas receives Life — becomes alive, gives back life and finally shows the relativity of nature.

Gradually, during the years he lived at Lavington, he reshaped the actual terrain surrounding him, digging, planting and creating ponds in a way that would have been familiar to Capability Brown who, much earlier, had undertaken a grander version of the same thing at nearby Petworth.

Hitchens's Top Works

- *Autumn Composition: Flowers on a Table, 1932*
- *Damp Autumn, 1941*
- *Terwick Mill No. 2, 1944*

HENRY JAMES
1 8 4 3 - 1 9 1 6

R Y E

Henry James was born in New York, and came from a well-known, and also wealthy, family of American intellectuals. His father, Henry senior, was a well-known figure among the Transcendentalists who were attracted by the personality and beliefs of Ralph Waldo Emerson; his brother was the philosopher William James. His formation as a writer was thoroughly cosmopolitan – he studied, at various times, in Geneva, London, Paris, Bologna and Bonn. He also spent a brief period at Harvard Law School.

His first European residence was Paris, where he sometimes wrote for the *New York Tribune*, but he soon moved to London, settling there in 1876. Of London he wrote, in 1888,

> *It is a real stroke of luck for a particular country that the capital of the human race happens to be British. Surely every other people would have it theirs if they could. Whether the English deserve to hold it any longer might be an interesting field of inquiry; but as they have not yet let it slip the writer of these lines professes without scruple that the arrangement is to his personal taste. For after all if the sense of life is greatest there, it is a sense of the life of people of our incomparable English speech.*

However, after more than 20 years, he decided he needed something more tranquil. He moved into Lamb House in Rye in 1898, and became a British subject in 1915, only shortly before his death. The characteristic products of his years in Rye are a group of elaborate late novels – *The Wings of a Dove* (1902), *The Ambassadors* (1903) and *The Golden Bowl* (1904). James's oblique fictional methods in these books drive some readers to distraction – his career has been bitchily described as consisting of three periods: James the First, James the Second, and James the Old Pretender. However the general view is that the late works are his most perfect products. Experts on James give the prize to *The Wings of a Dove*, although James himself, who was an excellent commentator on his own efforts, seems to have preferred *The Ambassadors*.

None of these books offers any reference to life in Sussex. Their settings are international and urban. The events recounted in *The Wings of A Dove* take place in London, then in Venice, and the central character is an American heiress. Rye was simply a place that offered James the seclusion he needed in order to write.

James's Top Works

- *Daisy Miller, 1879*
- *The Portrait of a Lady, 1881*
- *The Ambassadors, 1903*

RICHARD JEFFRIES
1 8 4 8 - 1 8 8 7

GORING-BY-SEA

The naturalist and novelist Richard Jeffries is generally thought of as a Wiltshire writer, since that was the county in which he was born and the place where the majority of his books are set, among them the children's story *Bevis* (*1882*), which holds its place as a minor classic. However he spent the last two years of his life in Sussex, living at Goring-by-Sea, and wrote powerfully about the Sussex countryside. There is a plaque to commemorate his residence there on the house he occupied, and it is a banal little building, with a banal name – Sea View.

Jeffries was already a very sick man when he came to live in Sussex, but he still had the eyes, and the strength, to write evocatively about it. Here is a typical passage:

The ancient forest land is still wild enough, there is no seeming end to the heath and fern on the ridges or to the woods in the valleys. These moor-like stretches bear a resemblance to parts of Exmoor. The oaks that once reached from here to the sea-shore were burned to smelt the iron in the days when Sussex was the great iron land. For charcoal the vast forests were cut down; it seems strange to think that cannon were once cast – the cannon that won India for us – where now the hops grow and the plough travels slowly, so opposite as they are to the roaring furnace and the ringing hammer. Burned and blasted by the heat, the ground where the furnaces were still retains the marks of the fire. But to-day there is silence; the sunshine lights up the purple heather and the already yellowing fern; the tall and beautiful larches stand graceful in the stillness. Their lines always flow in pleasant curves; they need no wind to bend them into loveliness of form: so quiet and deserted is the place that the wide highway road is green with vegetation, and the impression of our wheels is the only trace upon them. Looking up, the road – up the hill – it appears green almost from side to side. It is well made and firm, and fit for any traffic; but a growth of minute weeds has sprung up, and upon these our wheels leave their marks. Of roads that have become grass — grown in war — desolated countries we have all read, but this is our own unscathed England.

When Jeffries lived there Goring was fairly isolated, and had not yet acquired its full name. It was still just Goring. It became Goring-by-Sea when the railway finally reached it in 1906, as it was felt that there was a risk that it might now be confused with the better-known Goring-on-Thames, in Berkshire.

Jeffries's Top Works
- *Woods Magic: A Fable, 1881*
- *Bevis: the Story of a Boy, 1882*
- *After London, 1885*

DAVID JONES
1 8 9 5 - 1 9 7 4

DITCHLING

David Jones was born at Brockley in Kent, but throughout his life remained conscious of the Welsh heritage implied by his surname. His interest in art began early, encouraged by his mother, and in 1909, then aged 16, he enrolled in the Camberwell School of Art in London. Here he made his first contact with burgeoning Modernist ideas, as one of his teachers, A.S. Hatrick, had known Toulouse-Lautrec and Van Gogh in Paris, and had even passed some time in Pont-Aven with Gauguin. From another teacher, Reginald Savage, he learned about the work of Aubrey Beardsley (*see p.16*), and the elegant French Art Nouveau illustrator Maurice Boutet de Monvel. These were to be more lasting influences on Jones than the great Post-Impressionists.

In January 1915 Jones enlisted with the Royal Welch Fusiliers (the oldest Welsh regiment – the archaic spelling of the word 'Welch' derives from the fact it was founded as long ago as 1689), and spent the rest of World War I in their ranks. The war left an indelible mark on his psyche. When he was demobilized, he returned to art school, this time the Westminster School of Art. His search for the catharsis that would resolve the trauma of his war-time experiences led him first to Catholicism, then to Eric Gill's Guild of St Joseph and St Dominic at Ditchling. He joined Gill at Ditchling in 1921 (this is his connection with Sussex), and followed him to Capel-y-ffinn, where in 1924 he became engaged to Gill's daughter Petra, with whom her father had had an incestuous relationship. This engagement was broken off in 1927. In 1929 Jones was elected to the Seven and Five Society, a group which had begun its life in 1919 as a conservative reaction to what were seen as the excesses of Continental Modernism, but which in the mid-1920s was hijacked by Ben Nicholson and his associates, and which now espoused the Modernist cause. Among the other members were Barbara Hepworth, Henry Moore, Ivon Hitchens (*see p. 50*), Frances Hodgkins and John Piper. In the same year he started work on his epic poem about the war, *In Parenthesis*, which shows affinities with the work of William Blake (*see p. 24*) and also with the Celtic legendary narratives that he had always loved. In this he speaks of the way in which the horror of the war had to be at once avoided, accepted and absorbed:

> *Each variously averts his perceptions, makes the inward abysm.*

David Jones suffered a serious nervous breakdown in 1932, and stopped work for five years. *In Parenthesis* was finally published in 1937. In 1947 he suffered a further breakdown, but continued to work at both writing and painting, increasingly interesting himself in a fusion of the two. After breaking a hip in 1970, he retired into a nursing home, where he died in 1974.

Jones's Top Works

- *Manawydan's Glass Door*, 1932
- *In Parenthesis*, 1937
- *The Anathémata*, 1952

RUDYARD KIPLING
1 8 6 5 - 1 9 3 6

ROTTINGDEAN & BURWASH

Rudyard Kipling was born in 1865, in Bombay, India, where his father was a teacher of arts and crafts at the Jeejeebhoy School of Art. As the Indian climate was not considered healthy for English children, he was taken to England at the age of six, and placed in a foster home where he was deeply unhappy. In 1878 he entered United Services College in Devon, which prepared pupils for the army. Here he was happier but, because of his poor eyesight, and mediocre performance as a student, could not proceed to an army career.

In 1882 he returned to India to work as a journalist. Here he rapidly established a reputation as a poet and short-story writer. When he once again returned to Britain in 1889, he was already celebrated – some contemporary critics compared him to Dickens. In 1892, he got married, to an American, the sister of his best friend, and moved to the United States, but his attempt to settle there was not a success – he quarrelled with his brother-in-law and returned to Britain in 1896, settling first at Rottingdean in Sussex, then moving to Burwash in 1902, buying a beautiful 17th-century house called Bateman's, which is now preserved as a memorial to him. Much of his best work – *The Jungle Book (1894)*, *The Second Jungle Book (1895)*, and the mysterious adventure novel *Kim (1901)* – was produced during this restless period. During the first half of his life he firmly established his reputation as one of the chief spokesmen for Britain's imperial mission. This was to earn him many detractors after World War I, though his work never went completely out of favour, and found unexpected defenders among leading modernist intellectuals, chief among them T.S. Eliot.

When Kipling moved to Burwash his creative energy had already begun to decline. For some reason it declined still further when he was given the Nobel Prize for Literature in 1907, the first Englishman to receive it, and one of its youngest recipients. While the bulk of his writing is based on his experience abroad, particularly in India, there are two attractive late collections of poems and stories, ostensibly for children, which show his love for the place where he had settled. These are *Puck of Pook's Hill* (*1906*) and *Rewards and Fairies* (*1910*). Not all the material is specifically about Sussex, but some, such as the poem I quote here, definitely is, though it also mentions places in Kent:

> *I'm just in love with all these three,*
> > *The Weald and the Marsh and the Down countre.*
> *Nor I don't know which I love the most,*
> > *The Weald or the Marsh or the white Chalk coast!*
>
> *I've buried my heart in a ferny hill,*
> > *Twix' a liddle low shaw an' a great high gill.*
> *Oh hop-bine yaller an' wood-smoke blue,*
> > *I reckon you'll keep her middling true!*
>
> *I've loosed my mind for to out and run*
> > *On a Marsh that was old when Kings begun.*
> *Oh Romney Level and Brenzett reeds,*
> > *I reckon you know what my mind needs!*
>
> *I've given my soul to the Southdown grass,*
> > *And sheep-bells tinkled where you pass.*
> *Oh Firle an' Ditchling an' sails at sea,*
> > *I reckon you keep my soul for me!*

A THREE PART SONG, FROM PUCK OF POOK'S HILL

Kipling's Top Works
- *Jungle Book, 1894*
- *Kim, 1901*
- *Just So Stories, 1902*

HERBERT LA THANGUE
1859-1929

BOSHAM

Herbert La Thangue was one of those highly professional artists who tends to get left out of histories of British art, though to judge by the prices realised in the auction rooms, his work is still highly thought of by a number of wealthy collectors.

Born in London, he was educated at Dulwich College, the Lambeth School of Art and the Royal Academy Schools, where he was a great success. In 1879, at the age of 20 he was awarded a gold medal and a travelling scholarship. More important, Lord Frederick Leighton, who had been elected President of the Royal Academy in the preceding year, gave him a letter of introduction to Jean-Léon Gérôme, leader of the French classical school and sworn enemy of the Impressionists. La Thangue studied under Gérôme at the Ecole des Beaux Arts in Paris, which gave him an extremely solid technical foundation – more solid than that of nearly all his British contemporaries.

La Thangue was not, however, attracted to Gérôme's mixture of classicism and orientalism. What interested him was the work of the Barbizon school, and that of Jules Bastien-Lepage (*1848-84*), then nearing the end of his short life. Bastien-Lepage's 'realist' paintings of landscapes and peasant subjects – less realist, in fact, than the work of Courbet – were then immensely successful in France – he had been given the Legion of Honour in the year that La Thangue arrived in Paris. La Thangue spent the summers of 1881 and 1882 working with him in Britanny, and the experience left an indelible mark on his style. He also began to feel the influence of James Whistler, whose combative nature may have appealed to him though his style was never as radical as Whistler's own.

La Thangue returned to London in 1886 and tried to organize a revolt against the Royal Academy which proved to be abortive – and he continued to exhibit in the Academy's annual exhibitions. At first he lived in

Norfolk, painting scenes of fenland life in the Bastien-Lepage manner, and at the same time slowly building up a clientele amongst wealthy, new-rich mill owners in Yorkshire, who liked what they thought of as his no-nonsense style. Later he moved to Bosham in Sussex. Though some of his later paintings show Sussex scenes, he also travelled to Provence and Liguria. The work he did there was in part at least a reaction to his disillusionment at what was happening to rural life in England as the result of ever-increasing industrialization. It shows his awareness of, and interest in, French Impressionism without ever becoming fully Impressionist. The high point of his career was a one-man exhibition held at the Leicester Galleries in London, just before the outbreak of World War I, in which he showed a large number of these painting made in southern Europe. It was enthusiastically praised by Sickert, writing in the influential periodical *The New Age*.

After the war, La Thangue continued to paint in the same manner, with continuing financial success, but he was no longer a fashionable artist, having been overtaken first by Duncan Grant (*see p.44*) and other artists influenced by French Post-Impressionism, and later by Ben Nicholson and the circle surrounding him.

La Thangue's Top Works
- *Study in a Boatbuilding Yard on the French Coast, 1882*
- *Poverty, 1883*
- *The Man with the Scythe, 1896*

OLIVER MESSEL
1904-1978

NYMANS, HANDCROSS

Oliver Messel, together with Cecil Beaton, was the pre-eminent British theatrical designer of the 1930s, 1940s and 1950s. The grandson of a rich stockbroker of German-Jewish origin, he was brought up at the beautiful family estate at Nymans in Sussex. After schooling at Eton, where his contemporaries included Evelyn Waugh and Harold Acton, he went to the Slade School of Art in London. His original intention was to be a portrait painter, but his many contacts in the theatre meant that he was soon diverted into theatrical enterprises. His first commission was to design masks for the London production of *Zéphyr et Flore* (*1925*), a ballet choreographed by Massine for Diaghilev's Ballets Russes company. Admission to the Diaghilev circle automatically unlocked the doors to every artistic and social world he might wish to enter. Later he created costumes and sets for the C.B. Cochran reviews of the late 1920s and early 1930s, which showcased the words and music of Noel Coward.

The homosexual circle that Messel belonged to at this time was wittily satirized by the writer-composer Gerald Berners in a novella called *The Girls of Radclyffe Hall* (*1937*). This boarding-school farce parodies the naively emotional school stories written by the prolific Angel Brazil, while at the same time alluding to Radclyffe Hall's humourless lesbian novel *The Well of Loneliness (1928)*. Berners's friends are transformed into passionate female adolescents. Messel appears as 'Olive', and Beaton, who was bitterly jealous of his rival's professional and amorous success, is 'Cecily'. Messel was amused; Beaton decidedly not.

Messel's career continued successfully before, during and after World War II. He had now begun to receive commissions from the movie industry, beginning with costumes for Alexander Korda's *The Private Life of Don Juan* in 1934, and going on to work on other lavish spectacles, such as *The Thief of Baghdad* (*1940*) and *Caesar and Cleopatra* (*1946*). He also continued his connection with the ballet, designing a famous production of *The Sleeping Beauty* for Covent Garden in 1946. During the same period, in the years immediately after the war, he provided sets and costumes for the plays of Christopher Fry (*see p. 38*).

Perhaps his most publicized commission, however, was for a famous London hotel – the Oliver Messel Suite at the Dorchester, completed in 1953. It did not harm his reputation that this became the preferred residence of Elizabeth Taylor, whenever she happened to be in London. So well loved was it that it was meticulously refurbished and restored in 1981, under the supervision of Messel's nephew, Lord Snowdon.

Messel retired from the theatre in 1967, and went to live in Barbados, which had long been his holiday home. Here, and on one or two other West Indian islands, such as Mustique, he created, or else restored and extended, a group of lavish villas for his friends. When he died in 1974, his ashes were returned to England, and an elegant monument was raised to him in the beautiful garden of his childhood home, Nymans. This now belongs to the National Trust. The house itself was gutted by fire in 1947, and is preserved as a picturesque ruin.

Messel's Top Works
- *The Thief of Baghdad, film set design, 1940*
- *Suddenly, Last Summer, film set design, 1959*
- *Oliver Messel Suite, Dorchester Hotel, 1953*

Miller's Top Works (see next page)
- *The Lives of Lee Miller, Antony Penrose, 1985*
- *Lee Miller's War, ed. Antony Penrose, 1992*
- *The Legendary Lee Miller, Antony Penrose, 1998*

LEE MILLER
1907-1977

CHIDDINGLY

Lee Miller was an American – in her prime, a woman of extraordinary vivacity and beauty – whose reputation as a photographer has recently been experiencing a revival, thanks largely to the efforts of her son Anthony Penrose.

She was born in Poughkeepsie, NY, and her father, who was an engineer and camera enthusiast, taught her the basics of photography when she was still a child. At the age of seven she was raped by a family friend, who at the same time infected her with a venereal disease – this left psychological scars that took a long time to heal, if indeed they ever did. At 18 she went to Paris to study theatre design and lighting. On her return, a year later, she was spotted on a New York street by the magazine publisher Condé Nast, and through him became a successful fashion model, working for the leading American photographers of the time.

In 1929 she once more left for Paris, determined to meet the American photographer Man Ray. Ignoring his insistence that he did not take students, she soon installed herself as his assistant, mistress and model. Together they revived the photographic solarization process that became one of the hallmarks of Man Ray's style. According to the graphic account she gave much later to the curator and critic Mario Amaya,

> *Something crawled across my foot in the darkroom and I let out a yell and turned on the light. I never did find out what it was, a mouse or what. Then I quickly realised that the film was totally exposed: there in the development tanks, ready to be taken out, were a dozen practically fully-developed negatives of a nude against a black background. Man Ray grabbed them, put them in the hypo and looked at them later. He didn't even bother to bawl me out, since I was*

so sunk. When he looked at them, the unexposed parts of the negative, which had
been the black background, had been exposed by this sharp light that had been
turned on and they had developed, and came right up to the edge of the white,
nude body. But the background and the image couldn't heal together, so there
was a line left which he called a 'solarization'.

Through Man Ray, Miller met all the leading artists and intellectuals in
Paris, among them Picasso, the Surrealist poet Paul Eluard and Jean
Cocteau. In 1932 she returned to New York to set her own studio, but
this did not last long. In 1934 she married a rich Egyptian and went to
live with him in Egypt, but, still restless, returned to France in 1937,
where she met and began an affair with Roland Penrose, a wealthy
Englishman from a Quaker background. Penrose, a minor artist, but a
major patron of the arts, formed part of Picasso's entourage. Picasso
painted Miller during the month she and Penrose spent in his company
at Mougins in the South of France, and she made a number of photographs of the artist and his circle.

World War II provided the opportunity Lee Miller had been looking
for all her life, though perhaps without knowing it. She made pictures
of London in the Blitz, and in 1944 she became a combat photographer
– working rather incongruously for *Vogue* – and followed the allied
advance through France and into Germany, where she was present at
the liberation of Dachau and Buchenwald. The very direct photographs
she made during the war years are her best work.

She had not been faithful to Penrose during the war, but in 1946 she
divorced her Egyptian husband, and married him in 1947. The couple
settled at Farley Farm at Chiddingly, and entertained a wide spectrum
of celebrated friends there. Though Miller still occasionally took photographs of these visitors, she had essentially lost interest in photography
as an art, seemingly burned out by her wartime experiences. She now
became obsessed with cooking as a creative substitute, but at the same
time grew increasingly addicted to alcohol and Benzedrine. By the time
she died in 1977 she had completely lost her once astonishing beauty
but remained both fascinating and disconcertingly forthright to the end.

A.A. MILNE
1 8 8 2 - 1 9 5 6

ASHDOWN FOREST

lan Alexander Milne was born in London but became familiar with Sussex as a child. At the age of eight he wrote an article for his school magazine – his first published work – describing a walking tour in Ashdown Forest. In the early part of his career he worked in London, and afterwards as assistant editor for *Punch*. After serving in World War I in the Signal Corps he became a successful playwright – the best known of these plays being *Mr Pim Passes By*, produced in London in 1919, with Leslie Howard in the lead, and later in New York. It is a typical gentle drawing room comedy of the period, of a kind that now seems very dated.

Milne married in 1913, but his only child Christopher Robin was not born until 1920. In 1924, inspired by Christopher's presence in his life, Milne embarked on a career as a children's author, with a book of poems entitled *When We Were Very Young*. To illustrate the poems he called in his friend E.H. Shepard, a skilful illustrator who also worked for *Punch*. This book was followed by two celebrated books of children's stories, *Winnie the Pooh* (*1926*) and *The House at Pooh Corner* (*1928*), and another collection of poems for children, *Now We Are Six* (*1927*).

The character of Pooh was apparently based on a Canadian black bear named Winnipeg, which was the mascot of the Canadian regiment, the Royal Winnipeg Rifles, during World War I, and which was later given to the London Zoo. Shepard based his illustrations on his own childhood teddy-bear, Growler. Other characters, such as Kanga and Roo, were based on toys belonging to Christopher Robin. The setting is Ashdown Forest, where Milne acquired a house called Cotchford Farm in 1925, just as the first Pooh book was being written. He and Shepard spent many hours in the forest, looking for the right settings. Many of the locations in the Winnie the Pooh books are identifiable today.

Poohsticks Bridge, for example, is Posingford Bridge, built in 1907 and repaired in 1999 with funds from the Disney Corporation, to whom Milne's widow sold the rights for the series.

Curiously enough, however, Milne did not read the Pooh tales to his son, preferring to entertain him with the work of P.G. Wodehouse. The story, sadly, ends on a number of sour notes. Milne was violently and publicly indignant about Wodehouse's behaviour during World War II where, after being captured in France, he made a number of broadcasts on the German radio. After the war, Wodehouse retaliated by including parodies of Milne's children's poems in his later books. Milne's son Christopher found it a heavy burden that his father had used his real Christian names in the Pooh books and children's poems, and became partially estranged from his father, seldom visiting him after he had had a stroke in 1952, and never seeing his mother after his father's memorial service in 1956. This seems to have motivated her sale of the rights in Pooh to Disney in 1961.

Milne's Top Works

- *Winnie the Pooh, 1926*
- *Now We Are Six, 1927*
- *The House at Pooh Corner, 1928*

PAUL NASH
1 8 8 9 - 1 9 4 6

IDEN & RYE

P aul Nash is the best known of the artists who tried to ally elements borrowed from Surrealism with the British landscape tradition. He is best known for images produced during the two World Wars.

Nash was born in London, the eldest child of a successful barrister. His childhood was marked by a number of serious illnesses – he suffered from asthma. He was educated at Colet Court, the preparatory school for St Paul's school, then, having failed to pass his naval entrance examination, St Paul's itself, with art classes at Chelsea Polytechnic and later at the London County Council School in Bolt Court, off Fleet Street. In 1910 he went to the Slade School of Art, where he became friends with Ben Nicholson, the son of Sir William Nicholson (*see p. 70*), and the future leader of the inter-war avant-garde in Britain.

In 1914 he joined the Omega Workshops, founded by the Bloomsbury art-historian, critic and painter Roger Fry, and worked with Fry on the restoration of Mantegna's Triumphs in the Royal Collection at Hampton Court. On the outbreak of World War I he enlisted in the Artist's Rifles, but was not sent to France until 1917. After four months at the front and in reserve in the Ypres Salient, without seeing any serious fighting, he broke a rib in a fall and was sent back to England. At the end of October he returned to England and spent most of November there drawing the aftermath of the Battle of Passchendaele. The scenes he witnessed made an indelible impression on him, though he was disgusted and frustrated by the 'propaganda' aspect of his work. He said at the time:

> *I am no longer an artist. I am a messenger who will bring back word from the men who are fighting to those who want the war to go on forever. Feeble, inarticulate will be my message, but it will have a bitter truth and may it burn their lousy souls.*

On his discharge from the army in 1919 he lived first in London, then went to live at the coastal village of Dymchurch in Kent. In 1925 he moved with his wife to Iden in Sussex, then in 1931 to New House in Rye. In 1934, after nearly ten years' residence, he abandoned Sussex for Dorset, then moved back to London in 1936.

During the inter-war period he was active in the British art world, teaching briefly for two periods at the Royal College of Art, writing art criticism for *The Listener*, and serving as president and chairman of the Society of Industrial Artists.

In 1933 he was a founder-member of Unit One, perhaps the most influential group of progressive artists to appear in England in the inter-war period, and in 1936 he was a committee-member and also an exhibitor at the International Surrealist Exhibition held at the New Burlington Galleries in London. He also participated in International Surrealist Exhibitions in Tokyo (*1937*) and Paris (*1938*). During these years he was particularly fascinated by the strangeness and grandeur of Britain's prehistoric monuments.

In 1940 he was once again appointed as an Official War Artist, working now for the Air Ministry and the Ministry of Information. He died of pneumonia in July 1946.

Older than Eric Ravilious (*see p.74*), whom he briefly taught at the Royal College, and more deeply involved in avant-garde activity, Nash nevertheless has a number of things in common with him – a fascination with the clash between derelict or smashed items of machinery and apparently primeval landscapes, for example, and a desire to link the discoveries of Surrealism with things inherited from the English Romantic tradition, more specifically from William Blake and Samuel Palmer. Like Ravilious, Nash was a gifted book illustrator.

Nash's Top Works
- *We Are Making A New World, 1918*
- *Winter Sea (Dymchurch), 1925*
- *Battle of Britain, 1941*

SIR WILLIAM NICHOLSON
1 8 7 2 - 1 9 4 9

ROTTINGDEAN

William Nicholson was the son of an ironmaster from Nottinghamshire, who became a Conservative Member of Parliament. He received his artistic education first at a school run by the successful academic portrait painter Sir Herbert Herkomer (*1849-1914*) – he did not get on with Herkomer and left before he graduated – and later at the Académie Julian in Paris. The Académie was crowded with cosmopolitan students and offered a range of avant-garde influences, though little formal instruction. Nicholson, however, was hardly, if at all, influenced by the *fin-de-siècle* art then being made in Paris.

On his return to England he paired up with his fellow-artist and brother-in-law James Pryde to produce innovative posters based on the early 19th-century tradition of rough simplified woodcut illustrations for pamphlets of popular tales and ballads made to be sold in the streets. Soon after this Nicholson began producing woodcut prints in the same style. They called themselves the Beggarstaff Brothers. The most celebrated of these is his portrait of a dumpy and rather grumpy Queen Victoria, walking her dog. Other portrait prints from this time feature some of the major celebrities of the period.

Although his prints made him famous, Nicholson also began to make a career as a painter, producing portraits somewhat in the manner of James Whistler, and subtle still-life paintings that mingle the influences of Manet and Chardin. By 1909 he was prosperous enough to buy himself a holiday retreat at Rottingdean, and soon after this began painting exquisite landscapes of the South Downs that are amongst the finest images of Sussex scenery ever produced. These pictures are generally small, but through his use of simplified shapes, punctuated with tiny figures of grazing animals, Nicholson conveys a feeling of huge space and light. In a letter to *The Artist* in 1924, he attempted to describe how these effects were achieved. 'Simplification of tone,' he said 'is of great value', 'and the difference between color and tone is of equal importance. The knowledge of both these subjects adds enormously to sight enjoyment. Have you noticed how subconsciously grateful one feels to the masters for their simplification of line, tone and colour?'

In 1918 Nicholson's wife died in the great Spanish flu epidemic. Less than a year and a half later he married a rich second wife, Edith Stuart-Wortley, and moved with her to Sutton Verny in Wiltshire. In the post-war years he continued to paint in his now long-established manner which in the eyes of many people, including those of his son, had come to seem very old-fashioned. By 1933 he had separated from his second wife and had begun to work mostly in Spain. His new companion was the novelist Marguerite Steen. After the outbreak of the Spanish Civil War in 1936, they travelled together to other parts of Europe. In 1939 he suffered a stroke when visiting La Rochelle. Though he recovered partially from this, it affected his hand and eye co-ordination, and he did no painting in the last seven years of his life.

Nicholson had a rather tense and rivalrous relationship with his son Ben, who is currently much the more celebrated artist. However, Ben Nicholson was well aware that his father was his own precursor. Writing to Marguerite Steen in 1953, at a time when a catalogue raisonné of William's work was in the course of preparation, he said that his father's still-lifes and landscapes, 'were in my opinion universal, and it is this universality which endures and it is this which makes him a finer painter than any other British painter of his generation, except perhaps Sickert.'

Nicholson's Top Works
- *London Types, 1898*
- *Judd's Farm, 1912*
- *The Hundred Jugs, 1916*

THOMAS OTWAY
1652-1685

WOOLBEDING

Thomas Otway was the son of a Sussex clergyman, the rector of the church of All Hallows at Woolbeding. He was educated at Winchester College and Christchurch, Oxford, then moved to London at the age of 19, to try to make his fortune in the theatre. His first intention was to be an actor, but his first and only attempt at this, playing an old man in a revival of a play by Aphra Behn, was a disaster due to his crippling stage-fright:

> *Mr. Otway the Poet having an Inclination to turn Actor; Mrs. Behn gave him the King in the Play, for a Probation Part, but he being not us'd to the Stage; the full House put him to such a Sweat and Tremendous Agony, being dash't, spoilt him for an Actor.*

He therefore turned to writing plays. His first attempt, *Alcibiades* (*1675*) did not win him much reputation, but his second, the tragedy *Don Carlos* (*1676*), made him temporarily prosperous. It was based on a novel published four years earlier by the Abbé de Saint-Réal, which was used much later by Schiller for his own *Don Carlos*, and later still by Verdi (via Schiller) for the opera *Don Carlos*, now the best-known theatrical version of the story. Otway evidently had a good knowledge of French, as he followed *Don Carlos* with adaptations into English of Racine's *Bérenice* and Molière's *Les Fourberies de Scapin*.

These, in turn, were succeeded by a comedy, *Friendship in Fashion* (*1678*), which enjoyed a modest success at its first performance, but which was howled off the stage for its indecency when it was revived 30 years later – a sign of how much the cultural climate had changed in a relatively short space of time.

Unlike most of his rival Restoration dramatists, Otway is better known for his tragedies than for his comedies. The most celebrated and durable of these is *Venice Preserv'd* (*1682*), last revived in 1984 at the National Theatre in London. At the time of its first presentation this had strong topical interest because it seemed to allude to the atmosphere of fear about Catholic conspiracies fomented by Titus Oates. It also contained, in the character of the lecherous senator Antonio, a scathing portrait of the leading statesman Anthony Ashley-Cooper, 1st Earl of Shaftsbury, mistrusted by all factions for his frequent changes of side.

Otway's life was bedevilled by two things: first by his inability to make, or at least to hold on to money, and second by his unrequited love for the celebrated actress Elizabeth Barry, who had played the heroine Draxilla in Otway's *Alcibiades* at the age of 17. Generally agreed to be no great beauty, Barry enthralled many others, among them the aristocratic satirist John Wilmot, Earl of Rochester. She treated all these suitors badly, and Otway perhaps worst of all. Despairing, he wrote her one of the most touching love-letters in the English language:

> *Everything you do is a new charm to me, and though I have languished for seven long tedious years of desire, jealously despairing, yet every minute I see you I still discover something new and more bewitching. Consider how I love you; what would I not renounce or enterprise for you? I must have you mine, or I am miserable, and nothing but knowing which shall be the happy hour can make the rest of my years that are to come tolerable. Give me a word or two of comfort, or resolve never to look on me more, for I cannot bear a kind look and after it a cruel denial.*

Barry made no reply, and Otway did indeed die in misery. According to Theophilus Cibber's *Lives of the Poets*, published in 1753, he was reduced to begging for bread in the streets of London. Recognizing him, a former acquaintance gave him a guinea, instead of the penny he asked for. Otway rushed to buy a royal at a nearby baker's shop, and choked to death on the first bite.

Otway's Top Works

- *The Orphan, 1680*
- *Venice Preserv'd, 1682*
- *The Soldier's Fortune, 1683*

ERIC RAVILIOUS
1903-1942

EASTBOURNE

Eric Ravilious, like his contemporary Rex Whistler (*see p. 86*), lost his life in World War II. Both now seem typical of the artistic climate that prevailed in Britain between the wars. Born in London, Ravilious was brought up in Eastbourne. He studied first at Eastbourne School of Art, then studied at the Royal College of Art, where one of his teachers was Paul Nash (*see p. 68*). Afterwards, when in his early twenties, he taught part-time at the Eastbourne School of Art, before moving to share a house in Essex with his close friend Edward Bawden.

Though he remained in Essex after he married, he paid many return visits to Sussex – he was, like Sir William Nicholson (*see p. 70*) before him, particularly attracted by Sussex's downland landscapes, and also by the coastal scenery near the ferry port of Newhaven.

Ravilious was a watercolourist and a skilful maker of woodcuts and lithographs, rather than a painter in oils. He represents a kind of witty populism that allied itself to surrealism without ever committing itself fully to the international Surrealist Movement. Among his key influences were 19th-century popular prints, and the austerely elegant watercolours of the 18th-century artist Francis Towne. While his work is less baroque and fanciful that that of Whistler, and certainly much less so than that of Oliver Messel, he exists at a stylistic remove from the Modernism that flourished in Europe during the same period.

Like Whistler, he was a skilful muralist, but his murals, unlike Whistler's, have not survived. The most admired was made in collaboration with Bawden, for Morley College in London. This, painted between 1928 and 1930, was destroyed by bombing during the war.

In his early landscape work, Ravilious often made use of apparently derelict items of machinery. These reflect the agricultural depression that affected England during the inter-war years, but also enabled the artist to impart his chosen scenes with a feeling of contemporaneity, linked to a sense of alienation.

The visual devices he evolved for dealing with this kind of material proved ideally suited to his work as an Official War Artist. He was offered a six-month contract in 1939, and began work at Chatham in 1940. Later he was posted to the destroyer *H.M.S. Highlander*, and was a witness to the Battle of Norway, in which the British attempted, unsuccessfuly, to drive back the German invasion of Norway and Denmark. What excited him here were the scenery and light of the far north.

> *The grand thing, was going up into the Arctic Circle with a brilliant sun shining all night, Arctic terns flying by the ship — I simply loved it and in fact haven't enjoyed anything so much since the war.*

It was with this in mind that Ravilious engineered a visit to Iceland in 1942. Soon after his arrival he took part in an RAF search-and-rescue mission that took off from RAF Kaldadarnes, a remote airfield near the coastal town of Selfoss. The aircraft disappeared without a trace.

Ravilious's Top Works

- *Cuckmere Haven, 1929*
- *Downs in Winter, 1934*
- *Beachy Head, c. 1939*

THOMAS SACKVILLE
1536-1608

BUCKHURST

Thomas Sackville, 1st Earl of Dorset, was born at Buckhurst Park in Sussex, though in his later years he became more closely associated with Knole, the magnificent house he created in Kent. A lawyer from the Inner Temple and Member of Parliament from 1558, he was raised to the peerage by Queen Elizabeth I in 1567, taking the title Lord Buckhurst. In 1604 Elizabeth's successor, James I, made him an earl.

His rise into the upper ranks of Elizabethan functionaries was rapid. Elizabeth sent him on diplomatic missions to France and to the Low Countries (the only occasion when he fell into disfavour). In 1586 he was given the unpleasant task of telling Mary, Queen of Scots about her impending execution. He became Lord Treasurer in 1599 and Lord High Steward in 1601. After Elizabeth's death, James confirmed him in this position and gave it to him for life.

Sackville is chiefly remembered today for his share in writing *The Tragedie of Gorboduc* – the last two acts are his, the first three are by his collaborator Thomas Norton, the Queen's Chief Interrogator. First acted in 1561, it is the first blank-verse play in English, and the first tragedy in the language modelled on the Latin tragedies of Seneca – though, paradoxically, it takes its subject not from the classics, but from a remote period in British history. There are a number of parallels with the plot of Shakespeare's *King Lear*.

One prominent theme in the play is the need for a secure succession – always a touchy subject in Elizabeth's time. Written to be performed before the Queen at the Inns of Court, it seems at times ready to lecture the monarch directly:

This, this ensues, when noble men do faile
In loyall trouth, and subjectes will be kinges.
And this doth growe when loe unto the prince,
Whom death or sodeine happe of life bereaves,
No certaine heire remaines, such certaine heire,
As not all onely is the rightfull heire
But to the realme is so made knowen to be,
And trouth therby vested in subjectes hartes,
To owe fayth there where right is knowen to rest.

Elizabeth did not take this amiss. A couple of days after the first performance, she had the play repeated in the hall of her own palace.

⌒﹏

Sackville's Top Works
❂ *A Myrrour for Magistrates, ed. William Baldwin, 1559*
❂ *The Tragedie of Gorboduc, 1561*

PERCY BYSSHE SHELLEY
1792-1822

HORSHAM

One of the few major writers to have been born in Sussex, Shelley soon broke his links with the county. He was born at Field Place, near Horsham, the eldest son and heir of a wealthy and extremely conservative squire who was also the heir to a baronetcy. His grandfather, Sir Bysshe Shelley, allegedly enjoyed a reputation for miserly eccentricity.

Shelley was sent away to school when he was only ten years old, going first to Syon House Academy, then to Eton – a place he later equated with prison. In 1810 he enrolled as a student at University College, Oxford, but was expelled in the following year for writing a pamphlet called *The Necessity of Atheism*, written in conjunction with his friend Thomas Jefferson Hogg. The incident enraged his father, who visited him in London and insisted that he renounce both his friendship with Hogg and his radical political and social beliefs. Shelley refused and his father disinherited him. The estrangement became permanent when Shelley eloped to Scotland with the 16-year-old Harriet Westbrook, who was much below him in social class, since she was the daughter of the owner of a London coffee-house. At this point there began the wanderings that were to fill the rest of his life.

He went first to Ireland, to campaign for political reform there. In 1813, back in London, he met the radical philosopher William Godwin, and fell in love with Mary, Godwin's daughter by the pioneer feminist Mary Wollstonecraft. In a second elopement, Mary and Shelley moved to Switzerland in 1814, taking with them Jane (later called Claire) Clairmont, who was the daughter of the second Mrs Godwin. After a period in Geneva, where they consorted with Byron, who became Claire

Clairmont's lover, the group returned to London in 1816. In this year Shelley's wife Harriet drowned herself, and in December Shelley finally married Mary. Because of his radical beliefs, Shelley lost the custody of his two children by Harriet to her family.

In 1818 Shelley and Mary moved to Italy, where their two children, Clara and William died, and where another son, Percy Florence, was born. They once again formed part of the circle surrounding the charismatic personality of Byron. Byron had by this time fallen out with Claire Clairmont. Endeavouring to patch things up between them, Shelley travelled to Livorno. Returning by boat to La Spezia, Shelley and his companion Edward Williams were drowned in a sudden storm.

Shelley's major literary works, among them his masterpiece *Prometheus Unbound* (1820), were all produced during his last four years in Italy. Although his youngest sister Hellen (always spelt thus), from whom he parted when she was still a small child, later reported how much he had loved the Sussex countryside when he was a boy, its influence on his poetry, if it existed at all, was purely subliminal.

Shelley's Top Works

- *Prometheus Unbound, 1820*
- *Posthumous Poems, ed. M.B. Shelley, 1824*
- *A Defence of Poetry, 1840*

ROBERT TRESSELL
1870-1911

HASTINGS

Tressell was born Robert Noonan in Dublin, the illegitimate child of a retired senior member of the Royal Irish Constabulary, and was originally given his father's surname Robert Croker. He was the youngest of five children, from a stable but irregular union. At the age of 16, already in sympathy with radical working class ideas, he adopted his mother's surname, Noonan.

In 1888 he moved to South Africa, working first in Cape Town as a painter and decorator, then, after marrying and then separating from his wife, who was unfaithful to him, moved to Johannesburg in 1895. He divorced in 1897, obtaining custody of his only child, a daughter. In Johannesburg he became the Secretary of the Transvaal Federated Building Trades Council. He also joined the Executive Committee of the Centennial of 1798 Association, formed to commemorate the hundredth anniversary of the unsuccessful rebellion against British rule in Ireland led by Wolfe Tone and Lord Edward Fitzgerald. In this capacity Noonan led protests against the employment of skilled black labourers to prepare for the celebrations. In 1898 he also helped to form the Irish Brigade, a force that fought alongside the Boers when war with the British broke out a year later.

When the war began, Noonan did not join the fighting, but initially sat things out in a well-to-do suburb of Cape Town. He left South Africa in 1901, before the end of hostilities. On his return, he and his daughter settled in St Leonards, where one of his sisters was living. He continued to work as a decorator, but in less prosperous circumstances than previously. His energies were diverted into making designs for an airship. In 1905, he sent these to the War Office, having apparently forgotten his hostility to British military power. When they were rejected, he smashed his models and turned to left-wing politics once again. In

1906 he was dismissed, after a quarrel with his employer about taking too much time over a job, and began to find it difficult to get work. It was then that he began to write *The Ragged Trousered Philanthropists*, now celebrated for its depiction of the lives and working conditions of the early 20th-century working class. He chose the pen-name 'Tressell' as an allusion to the trestle-table used by professional decorators.

The original manuscript was 1600 pages long, and was rejected by three publishers after it was completed in 1908. Depressed, Noonan tried to burn it, but it was rescued by his daughter Kathleen. Noonan had been suffering from tuberculosis since 1907, and now decided to emigrate to Canada to make a new life. He died in Liverpool Workhouse Infirmary while waiting to embark.

His daughter finally got a version of the novel published in 1914, with much of the socialist ideology cut out. This truncated version was a worldwide success, appearing in America and Canada the same year, in Russia in 1920 and in Germany in 1925. It has now sold over a million copies. A full edition was not published until as late as 1955. Despite the fact that its basic story is that of the betrayal of the socialist ideal, it is still regarded as a kind of primer of socialist ideas. Some people credit it with playing a significant part in the landslide victory of the Labour Party in the parliamentary election of 1945.

The setting for the story is St Leonards and Hastings ('Mugsborough'), where Noonan spent the last years of his life. It is therefore at least as intimately connected with Sussex as the rural idylls produced by other Sussex authors. Its first publisher Grant Richards, who bought the rights for £25, said of it ruefully:

The book was damnably subversive but extremely real.

That verdict is still valid today.

Tressell's Top Work
❯ *The Ragged-Trousered Philanthropists, 1914*

J . M . W . T U R N E R
1 7 7 5 - 1 8 5 1

P E T W O R T H

J oseph Mallord William Turner was the son of a London barber.
From his earliest childhood he was obsessed with art, and acquired
a reputation as a child prodigy when he had a painting accepted for
exhibition at the Royal Academy at the age of only 15. By the time
he was 18 he had established his own studio, and in 1802, when still in
his 20s, he was elected a full Royal Academician.

Secretive and solitary, Turner made many journeys both in England
and on the continent, seeking subject matter for his art. More and more
he tended to depict this, not in terms of strict topographical accuracy,
but in those of his own emotional state. Certain locations, however,
became special to him, and one of these was the great Sussex mansion
of Petworth, where he was a frequent guest between 1828 and 1837, and
where the owner, George Wyndham, the 3rd Earl of Egremont, had a
studio set up for him in a room called the Old Library.

The aristocratic owners of Petworth had long been renowned as
patrons of art. The picture collection was founded in the 1630s by the
10th Earl of Northumberland, a patron of Van Dyck. Having passed
through the female line, the estate was inherited in 1763 by the 3rd Earl
of Egremont. During his long reign at Petworth, Lord Egremont was
an enthusiastic patron of the contemporary art of his day, buying work
by Reynolds, Gainsborough, Zoffany and Fuseli. Turner was his particular favourite, and some 20 paintings by him now remain in the house.
No other place in England is as closely associated with him. The majority of these works represent the place itself – they are superb panoramic
paintings of the park, which had been designed by Capability Brown for
Lord Egremont's father. The most radical painting Turner made at
Petworth is not a landscape but an interior, the *Interior at Petworth* (now
in the collection of Tate Britain in London), which dates from circa 1837,

the very end of the artist's time there. Here all the forms of a palatial room are dissolved by a great onrush of light.

As Susan Sidlaukas wrote in her study of this work:

> The interior at Petworth is an unprecedented conflation of Romantic landscape and domestic architectural interior. The room's structural frame – with its wide golden moldings – appears intact. But rays of orange and yellow light and an overlapping curtain of emerald sweep through the room with a freedom that emphasizes its exposure and abandonment. This interior, desolate and disordered, is generally believed to express Turner's grief over the death in 1837 of George Wyndham, the third earl of Egremont, and lord of Petworth House in Sussex. The room Turner depicted here is in part a synthesis of the actual spaces and decor at Petworth – or at least the artist's representations of them. But conspicuous elements in the painting diverge so significantly from the circumstances of Petworth and its owner that they assert the presence of a conception that transcends literal references to time or place.

In addition to finished paintings, Turner made a great mass of studies at Petworth in watercolour and gouache, portraying the interior spaces as often as the exterior. In the gouaches he uses a blue paper as the ground, instead of the more usual white, to enhance the glow of his chosen hues. These works are the most daring works of art made in Sussex during the 19th century, when leading British artists were most active there. It is fascinating to note that they stand at the very beginning of this epoch of artistic activity, rather than towards its end.

Turner's Top Works

❯ *Brighton Chain Pier, c. 1828*

❯ *Petworth Park with Tillington Church in the Background, 1828*

❯ *Interior at Petworth, c. 1837*

H.G. WELLS
1 8 6 6 - 1 9 4 6

MIDHURST

One of the most popular authors of his time, Herbert George Wells had two important links with Sussex. Though he was born in Kent, his mother worked as a house-keeper at the great West Sussex mansion of Uppark from 1880 to 1893. She had previously been a maid at Uppark and Wells's father was a gardener there when the couple met. Though she was not supposed to have any of her children to live with her, Wells was frequently at the house, and was allowed to use the extensive library – something that greatly helped his intellectual development.

At the age of 15, Wells served one of several apprenticeships in different trades at a chemist shop in Midhurst. His other apprenticeships (all of which were equally unsuccessful) were with two drapers' shops, one of them in Windsor, the other in Southsea. To reach his place of employment in Midhurst he had to walk there from Uppark, which was a trek of 29 kilometres every day.

Before he lost his job in Midhurst, because his mother could no longer afford to pay for his training, Wells began to learn Latin, in order to be able to read and write up prescriptions. This extra work made the journey from Uppark too much of a burden, and he lodged in Midhurst with the man who was his teacher and who was also headmaster of the local grammar school. Later, after losing the second of his draper jobs, Wells wrote to the headmaster, and got a job there as a student teacher, taking classes by night to broaden his own education. His mentor steered him away towards science. Wells's time in Midhurst is now commemorated by no fewer then three commemorative plaques – one at his lodgings, one at the chemist's where he worked and one at the grammar school.

Wells was eventually awarded a scholarship at London University's Normal School of Science in South Kensington, where he studied a range of subjects, among them zoology, and biology (with the great Victorian scientist T.H. Huxley – at that time the leading exponent of Darwin's theory of evolution) and geology. When Huxley left, his enthusiasm for his classes waned and he left without a degree, but his education at South Kensington left an indelible mark on his writing.

Wells is now best remembered as one of the inventors of the modern literary genre of science fiction. Among his best known books are *The Time Machine* (1895), *The Invisible Man* (1897) and *The War of the Worlds* (1898), all written at the start of his career. A less-known book, *The World Set Free* (1914) predicts the invention of the atomic bomb.

Wells's Top Works

- *The Time Machine, 1895*
- *The War of the Worlds, 1898*
- *The Invisible Man, 1897*

REX WHISTLER
1905-1944

BRIGHTON

Rex Whistler was a charming and charismatic member of the upper-class social set known as the Bright Young Things in the 1920s, and their successors in the 1930s. He studied first, unsuccessfully, at the Royal Academy Schools , from which, as he later said, he was 'sacked for incompetence', and later at the Slade. In 1927, aged only 22, he was commissioned to paint elaborate mural decorations for the restaurant of the Tate Gallery, now Tate Britain. These established him as a leading exponent of the revived Rococo style which became fashionable in Britain in the inter-war years, as an alternative to Modernism, though with certain elements borrowed from the international Surrealist movement. He went on to paint murals for a number of large country houses, among them Plas Newydd and Dorneywood. He also made posters for Shell and designs for Wedgwood china. In 1935, he created a design for a huge carpet featuring the sea-god Neptune for West Dean Park, in Sussex, for the wealthy aesthete Edward James.

Whistler's real association with Sussex, however, belongs to the war years, when he was in the army, and stationed in Bosham and Brighton before the invasion of Normandy. Today his best known work is his delicious comic allegory *The Prince Regent Awakening the Spirit of Brighton*, originally painted on the wallpaper of a room in 39 Preston Park Avenue, Brighton, where the artist was then billeted. It is now housed in the Royal Pavilion. Rex Whistler was killed in action in July 1944, shortly after the D-Day landings.

Whistler's Top Works

◉ *Tate Gallery Café Mural, 1927*

◉ *Neptune Carpet, 1935*

◉ *Allegory: HRH The Prince Regent Awakening the Spirit of Brighton, 1944*

LEONARD WOOLF
1 8 8 0 - 1 9 6 9

RODMELL

Leonard Woolf's reputation has been over-shadowed by that of his more famous wife, Virginia, and in recent years some feminist writers have even tried to demonize him as a controlling male presence who actually exploited her, financially and emotionally, rather than looking after her. As her suicide note proves, this does not appear to have been her own view.

Born in London, he was the third of ten children. His father was a Jewish barrister who died when his son was quite young. Woolf was educated at a boarding school near Brighton and then at St Paul's in London. He won a scholarship to study classics at Trinity College, Cambridge, where he got to know the group of young men who were to form the nucleus of the Bloomsbury Group, among them Thoby Stephen, Virginia's brother.

In 1904 he became a cadet in the Ceylon Civil Service, going first to Jaffna, where he acquired a reputation for arrogance – so much so that the people of the town held a mass meeting to request that he be trans-ferred. This incident seems to have triggered a revulsion in Woolf against the whole imperialist-colonialist culture. His nephew by marriage, Quentin Bell, later said of him:

> It would be wrong to think of him as one so cerebral in his approach to life
> as to be quite separated from his fellows by a 'superior' Cambridge arrogance…
> If he ever had that quality, he lost it in Ceylon.

In May 1911 Woolf returned to London, supposedly for a year's leave. Instead he resigned after a few month's thought, and married Virginia Stephen in 1912, binding himself forever to Bloomsbury culture. He began writing novels — *The Village and the Jungle*, based on his experiences in Ceylon, appeared in 1913.

When World War I broke out, Woolf was rejected by the military, and therefore did not have to register as a conscientious objector. His thoughts increasingly turned to politics and sociology. He became a member of the Fabian Society, joined the Labour Party and began to write for the left-wing weekly review the *New Statesman*.

He also began a small publishing enterprise, at first purely as a hobby to distract his wife from her enveloping depression. Called the Hogarth Press, after their then house in Richmond, Hogarth House, this gradually became one of the more distinguished publishers of the inter-war period, with a list that included T.S. Eliot, Robert Graves, Christopher Isherwood, Katherine Mansfield and E.M. Forster, in addition to the Woolfs themselves. In the same period he was also very active as the editor of a series on influential literary and political periodicals.

Soon after Virginia Woolf's suicide he formed a relationship with Trekkie Parsons, a South African-born illustrator married to Ian Parsons, one of the directors of Chatto & Windus, which had swallowed up the Hogarth Press. The three of them settled into a curious *ménage à trios* in which Trekkie lived with him during the week and with her husband at the weekends. Given the general complication of Bloomsbury amorous and marital arrangements, this was less strange than it might have been in a different context. Trekkie was his residuary legatee when he died in 1969, and it was through her that Monk's House reached Sussex University and was then passed to the National Trust.

Leonard Woolf was a long surviving custodian, not only of his wife's literary legacy but of Bloomsbury values. He famously said,

> *Anyone can be a barbarian; it requires a terrible effort to*
> *remain a civilized man.*

Woolf's Top Works

◉ *The Village and the Jungle*, 1913
◉ *After the Deluge*, 1931-51
◉ *Principia Politica*, 1953

VIRGINIA WOOLF
1 8 8 2 - 1 9 4 1

RODMELL

Virginia Woolf is now perhaps the best-known Sussex author, thanks to her long residence at Monk's House at Rodmell. She was the daughter of Sir Leslie Stephen, the first editor of the *Dictionary of National Biography*, and Julia Duckworth. Both parents had been married before. Her mother already had three children – two sons and a daughter – by her previous marriage; Leslie Stephen had a daughter.

A series of family dramas and tragedies marked her adolescence and early adult years. Her two half-brothers sexually abused her, further traumatizing an already fragile nature. Her mother died in 1895, precipitating the first of many breakdowns. Her half-sister Stella Duckworth died in 1897, leaving Virginia's older full sister Vanessa (who was to become the painter Vanessa Bell, *see p.18*) in charge of the household.

In 1904 Sir Leslie Stephen died, and Vanessa, Virginia and their two brothers Thoby and Adrian formed a new household at Gordon Square in Bloomsbury. This rapidly became a social centre for the brilliantly intelligent friends Thoby brought home from Cambridge, where he was now a student. Among them were Lytton Strachey, Clive Bell and Leonard Woolf (*see p.87*), who differed somewhat from the rest of the group because he was Jewish. It was at this time that Virginia took her first steps as a writer.

In 1906 Thoby died of typhoid, contracted while on holiday in Greece. This precipitated Vanessa's marriage to Clive Bell, which did not please Virginia, who had envisaged living permanently with her sister.

The Gordon Square household now split up and after an interval Virginia found herself sharing quarters with her brother Adrian, John

Maynard Keynes the economist, Duncan Grant (*see p.44*), who at that point was Keynes's lover, and Leonard Woolf, newly returned from a spell as a colonial administrator in Ceylon (now Sri Lanka). It was at this point that Virginia also began using small houses in Sussex as holiday homes – first Little Talland House at Firle, then Asheham House near Lewes (now demolished). She contemplated marrying Lytton Strachey, although she knew he was homosexual, but this came to nothing. In January 1912, Leonard Woolf, who was 'sick of being an imperialist', proposed to her, and in May of that year she accepted him. They were married in August and the following month she had a major breakdown and attempted suicide, but was saved by a quick-thinking doctor.

In many ways the alliance with Woolf was a strange one. Though he was, on the surface of things at least, a fully integrated member of the Bloomsbury clan, he was also an outsider. While he was in Ceylon, his Cambridge friend Lytton Strachey fantasized about him as a kind of dangerous barbarian:

> *[Woolf] trembled all over, he was so violent, so savage; he had pulled his thumb out of joint in a dream; he was in short a serious and powerful figure; but he had gone off to live in a jungle and no one knew whether he would ever return.*

Virginia herself was frankly anti-Semitic. Much later, she said:

> *How I hated marrying a Jew – how I hated their nasal voices and their noses and their wattles.*

It seems to have been agreed from the beginning that the marriage would be sexless. Virginia's emotional ties, outside of marriage, were always with women. In the 1920s she had a very open lesbian affair with the poet Vita Sackville-West, celebrated in her charming historical fantasy *Orlando* (*1928*). By this time the Woolfs were dividing their time between London and Rodmell, where they bought Monk's House in 1919. They did not make Rodmell their exclusive residence until 1940, after the outbreak of World War II.

In the inter-war years, Virginia Woolf produced a series of brilliant novels, which established her as one of the foremost experimental writers of the period. Throughout this period she was fighting her depression, and Sussex was the place where she found it easiest to write, though she never became fully part of the local community, which regarded her as being distinctly eccentric. Dirk Bogarde (*see p.26*), who was brought up nearby, remembered seeing her out walking:

> She was tall and thin, with a long woolly, and fairish hair which looked as if she had just washed it.

He also remembered a childhood friend of his remarking:

> Londoner. From over there in Rodmell... They say she's a bit do-lally-tap. She writes books... Always up and down the river she is, like a bloomin' witch.

As the war continued, her depressions became more and more serious. On March 28th 1941 she filled her pockets with stones, and drowned herself in the River Ouse. For her husband Leonard, she left behind a touching letter:

> I feel certain that I am going mad again. I feel we can't go through another of those terrible times. And I shan't recover this time. I begin to hear voices, and I can't concentrate. So I am doing what seems the best thing to do. You have given me the greatest possible happiness. You have been in every way all that anyone could be. I don't think two people could have been happier till this terrible disease came...

Her body was not discovered until three weeks after her suicide. She was cremated and her ashes were scattered in the garden of Monk's House, which now belongs to the National Trust.

Woolf's Top Works
- *Mrs Dalloway*, 1925
- *To the Lighthouse*, 1927
- *Orlando*, 1928

W. B. YEATS
1865-1939

ASHDOWN FOREST & STEYNING

William Butler Yeats was born in Dublin, to a prominent Anglo-Irish Protestant family. His father, John Butler Yeats, was a celebrated but improvident artist. Yeats himself is now firmly established as one of the greatest of Irish 20th-century writers. Nevertheless he always retained roots in the English literary world. Though his first volume of verse appeared in 1887, in his early period of activity he was chiefly known as a playwright – in partnership with Lady Gregory he founded the Irish Theatre (later to become the Abbey Theatre), which was the flagship of the whole Irish nationalist literary revival. He remained its chief playwright until the appearance of John Millington Synge.

Around 1910, Yeats's writing began to take on a much tougher and less dreamy, though not less mystical tone. His transformation into a leading Modernist writer nevertheless took some time to accomplish.

Two crucial episodes in Yeats's life are linked to Sussex. In the winters of 1913 to 1916, Yeats spent time in Stone Cottage, in Ashdown Forest, with the much younger American poet Ezra Pound. The two men had a profound effect on each other's work. Although Pound was ostensibly Yeats's employee, and worked as his secretary, it was in reality a conversation between equals. Pound coaxed Yeats into tightening and hardening his style, as can be seen in the collection he published in 1914, significantly entitled *Responsibilities*, while Yeats introduced Pound to certain aspects of mystical or magical thinking. Yeats was also excited by the Japanese Noh plays that Pound was then editing.

The 1920s were years of glory for Yeats. He was appointed to the Irish Senate in 1922 and given the Nobel Prize in 1923. He is said to have been one of the very few Nobel prize-winners whose best work was produced after, rather than before, the award. During these years he both resisted and celebrated the ageing process, expressing his wish to be a 'wild, wicked old man'. Although now successfully married to Georgie Hyde-Lees after his long, frustrating courtship of the beautiful Maude Gonne, Yeats had several mistresses in his later years. In the last months of his life Yeats paid a visit to one of them, Edith Shackleton Heald, at Chantry House in Steyning, which now carries a plaque commemorating his association with the place. Here he made the preliminary prose draft for his final play, *The Death of Cuchulain*, which is also his own farewell to life. Edith was later present at his death in Roquebrune in 1939. In 1940 she moved in with the lesbian painter Gluck (Hannah Gluckstein, *1895-1978*) with whom she shared her life until her own death in 1976.

Yeats' Top Works
- *The Wind Among the Reeds, 1899*
- *Michael Robartes and the Dancer, 1921*
- *Last Poems, 1936-1939*

INDEX